Goddess Wheel of the Year

Also by Katherine MacDowell

Neopagan Theology Series

Ethics & Professional Practice for Neopagan Clergy
Sacred Groves: Creating and Sustaining Neopagan Covens
Ritual & Liturgy for Wiccan Clergy

-

Additional Works

Witness: A Collection of Poetry
Vestiges & Bones

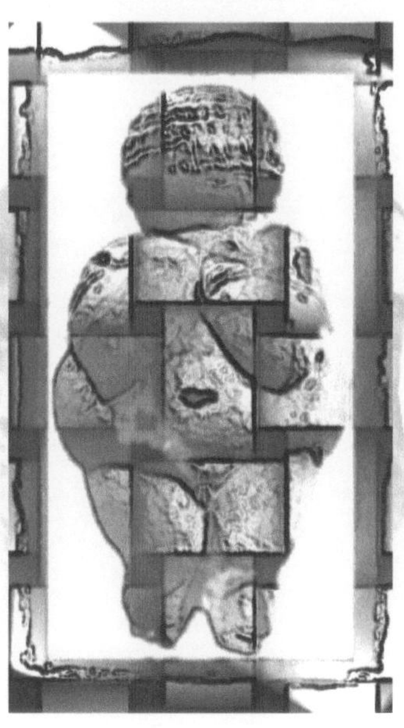

Goddess Wheel of the Year

Katherine MacDowell
D.DIV., D.TH., MA, M.ED., SH., HP., OCP

Ocean Seminary College
Lulu Press

For further information, please write to:
Ocean Seminary College Press
OSCPress@OceanSeminaryCollege.org

Published by Lulu
North Carolina, USA
www.Lulu.com

Second Edition

ISBN: 978-0-557-36350-6

Dedicated to the collective spirit and wisdom of

the Virgins, Mothers, Crones;

the Sacred Feminine who co-create the world.

Contents

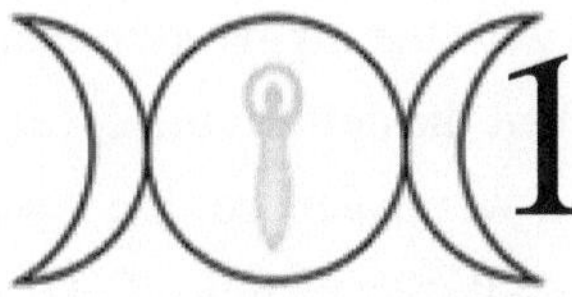

The year is a dancing woman who is born at the coming spring.
The year is a dancing woman; of her birth and death we sing.
—Shekhinah Mountainwater

The Goddess Wheels

The Dancing Woman: A Retelling

Known as Gaia, Ge, Gaea, and Eurynome, she is the Creatrix who danced the world from chaos. She rose up from the depths of the eternal space of nothing and finding no place to rest her feet, she danced and divided the waters from the heavens. And in the wake of her dance the North Wind blew and she grabbed it to her and created the great serpent Ophion, her companion. And she and Ophion danced and merged. And after the merging, Eurynome transformed herself into a great gull and floated upon the waves. And upon the vast ocean, she laid an egg. And her companion Ophion circled the Universe, the Great Cosmic Egg, keeping it warm and secure, until it soon hatched. And from within the depths of the Great Egg, the Universe was born. Out sprang the many children of Eurynome: the planets, the stars, the moons, and the very life and landscape of the Earth itself. And Ophion, the giant serpent, known also as Jörgmungandr[1], forever encircles the universe, nurturing the life that Eurynome, the Mother of All, continues to dance and keep in rhythm.

❀

Human history is filled with the myths, sacred artwork, and celebrations of the Goddess. Even when the cults of the Great Mother in the Near East and the Western World were silenced, the voice of the Divine Mother remained vibrant in non-Western cultures and would soon find a vocal space in Christianity, rising from beneath churches situated upon on ancient temples sites in the lives of saints and in the rise of the Cult of the Virgin Mary. In the 20th century, the Divine Mother, Her Sisters, Daughters, and Grandmothers have once more reemerged as the cornerstone of increasingly vocal and revitalized Neopagan faiths. With her consort, she is the principle figure of power, guidance, and inspiration to Wiccans worldwide; and to the growing movement of Goddess worshippers, she is parthogenesis[2] personified—the sole bringer of Life and Death, Creation and Sustenance—whole unto herself. She is the dancing goddess who keeps life in motion, ever creating, in a rhythmic cycle. This growing Goddess-centered focus on faith requires finding new ways to honor and celebrate the Goddess. In this book, we'll be looking her dance and how to create a Goddess-centered year of danceful worship to help you and your faith-based community to increase your closeness and act as conduits for her creative and sustaining power with the Divine Virgin–Mother–Crone.

A Year of Worship, A Year of Dance

Religions worldwide are marked by a constellation of sacred days. Days linked to myth and meaning; days that emerged to help adherents focus their attention toward the Divine in their lives. While we all know that faith must extend to our everyday lives, sacred or holy days provide us with important experiences to help affirm and reaffirm our faiths. Keeping a sacred calendar provides us with:

- the opportunity to celebrate in a community with shared rituals and goals, thus increasing our sense of connectedness to others while reinforcing our faith; these communal celebrations in turn help to establish tradition and expand upon the theological elements of our faith;

- the capacity to regenerate our energy and break from distress by setting aside time outside of our everyday life to focus on prayer and ritual;
- the opportunity to centralize our focus on our relationship with the divine to facilitate greater deepening of this relationship;
- numerous opportunities to sanctify our lifecycle experiences and symbolically locate them within the greater cycles of birth, death and rebirth of the divine;
- in the case of magical-based traditions, opportunities to enhance our magical work to help us bring the full power of the divine into our life and goals; and
- opportunities to reflect upon how we manifest our faith in our day-to-day lives and explore ways to better merge our daily life with our religious one.

Goddess-based worship does not manifest any differently in the function of sacred days as other religions. Sacred days are opportunities for us to align ourselves with high-points of energy—days held sacred to both the Goddess and humans alike. Within Goddess traditions sacred days are celebratory, even in the face of death. Birth and death provide us opportunities to share in the same life events as the Goddess herself experiences. She continuously creates the world through her cycles of birth, growth, death and rebirth. And, we, as expressions of and containers for her creative power, our own births, developments, deaths, and eventual rebirths actively contribute to the co-creation of the world. Our sacred calendars intrinsically reflect, not only these broad cycles of creation, but also serve to provide us with opportunities to bring into the world the Goddess's creative power. Within Goddess Traditions, each individual is simultaneously the created and the creator/tress. We encounter sacred days as opportunities to ask contribute our own energy to the flow of the universe.

☽ ○ ☾

A Year of Worship, A Year of Dance

Religions worldwide are marked by a constellation of sacred days. Days linked to myth and meaning; days that emerged to help adherents focus their attention toward the Divine in their lives. While we all know that faith must extend to our everyday lives, sacred or holy days provide us with important experiences to help affirm and reaffirm our faiths. Keeping a sacred calendar provides us with: the opportunity to celebrate in a community with shared rituals and goals, thus increasing our sense of connectedness to others while reinforcing our faith; these communal celebrations in turn help to establish tradition and expand upon the theological elements of our faith. Goddess-based worship does not manifest any differently in the function of sacred days as other religions. Sacred days are opportunities for us to align ourselves with high-points of energy—days held sacred to both the Goddess and humans alike. Within Goddess traditions sacred days are celebratory, even in the face of death. Birth and death provide us opportunities to share in the same life events as the Goddess herself experiences. She continuously creates the world through her cycles of birth, growth, death and rebirth. And, we, as expressions of and containers for her creative power, our own births, developments, deaths, and eventual rebirths actively contribute to the co-creation of the world. Our sacred calendars intrinsically reflect, not only these broad cycles of creation, but also serve to provide us with opportunities to bring into the world the Goddess's creative power. Within Goddess Traditions, each individual is simultaneously the created and the creator/tress. We encounter sacred days as opportunities to ask contribute our own energy to the flow of the universe.

☽ ○ ☾

The Wheel

Within the traditions of the Goddess, we call the yearly celebration cycle a "Wheel"—reflecting an eternal, ever-turning cycle that has no beginning and no end. This further reinforces an underlying central thealogy[3] of Goddess traditions that for every ending is a birth and for every beginning there is an ending. Both of these reflect an intimately connected and ever-present cycle made visible throughout the year in Nature's cycles[4].

In the Goddess traditions there are several interconnected wheels, in fact most Goddess paths create diagrams that interlock each of these cycles into a unified, broad whole[5] typically envisioned as a spiral. The spiral is further contained within the Goddess—literally within the womb of the Goddess. As such, we can deepen our understanding of the Goddess's Wheel of the Year as a process of the Goddess gestating and

> ☽○☾ **Symbol & Ritual Tip**
>
> Within the imagery of the umbilical cord or a ball of sacred thread unwinding, we encounter a potentially potent image to incorporate within ritual experience. We may utilize this object to track the holy days of the year, unfolding the thread at each sacred day, marking the development of the Goddess. Optionally, you could bless a yarn of thread (for those who spin, this can be a potent way of creating a sacred object as spinning is symbolic of the Goddess as weaver of fates and life) and unfold it each day with a prayer to the Goddess.

birthing various cycles in our world. These cycles spin forth from her like an umbilical cord linking her to us or as Ariadne's thread that unwinds into the labyrinth. The cycles unfurl until the Goddess, herself, is

☽ ○ ☾

unwound into a kind of nothingness or death-state where she must ultimately rebirth herself, recreating the sacred cord.

Within the unfolding of the year, we encounter her simultaneously in her nurturing aspect, as the One Who Ever-Procreates, and in her death aspect, as the One Who Ever-Receives. In Goddess Traditions, there are numerous wheels spiraling together that can be honored during a year and these broad cycles are: (a) Lunar, (b) Harvest, (c) Solar, (d) Seasonal, (e) Mythic, and (f) Developmental. These cycles each contain a wide range of internal possibilities for creative expression and, in many traditions, these broad cycles are interconnected, seen as each illuminating a facet of the goddess. Let's now turn to look at each of these cycles individually.

The Lunar Dance

Lunar cycles are common in most Neopagan traditions, whether they hold a Goddess and God as the center of the cosmology or a Goddess alone. In these contemporary traditions the lunar time is seen as the domain of the Goddess[6]. It is a time that is intimately connected to the flowing of liquids, whether the ocean (the lifeblood of the planet) or a woman's menstrual cycle (the lifeblood of the human species). The Lunar Wheel is the visible, pre-Julian monthly cycle and thus the natural method of keeping time. Further, the Lunar Wheel still remains the primary method by which nonhuman animals (particularly ocean-dwelling) align their migratory and procreative cycles.

The broad Lunar Wheel is tracked via the 13 full moons that occur during a yearly cycle. During which time, gathering in communal worship or engaging in private work is common. There is a wide range of variation in terms of the meaning of each of these moon cycles ranging from a Celtic Tree system or US-based folk traditions to more contemporary Goddess interpretations, such as those explored by Z Budapest in *Grandmother Moon.*

☽ ○ ☾

☽○☾ Symbol & Ritual Tip

I generally recommend students forgo the textbooks and determine the unique meaning of each cycle by to taking a 13-lunarmonth journey by observing the natural cycles in the ecological system they live within. This will help you discover just what Dance the Great Mother spins in nature each month within your home area. It will also help you identify what kind of energy is most strong during which moon month. Knowing what broad cycle of meaning is becoming manifest in your area will allow you to create a personal and meaningful set of rituals that link you directly to the Great Mother's energy. Further, once you have discovered the lunar themes of time in your home area, you can begin to sense the shifting aspects of the Great Mother and work with specific goddess energy that is emerging.

Additionally, within the Lunar Wheel, you have a further option to refine your monthly worship into two variant cycles best identified as the Triple Goddess Moon Wheel. These are best for solitary work as it requires a more substantial time investment in the monthly worship schedule (three times a month versus once a month). Nevertheless working within these variants does allow you to focus your observations in the world around you with even more precision.

Variant 1

This moon wheel begins with the waxing moon—the moon that builds after the Dark Moon[7]. This is the Maiden. During this particularly time, ritual work may be directed toward deepening connection to a Maiden Goddess or working on issues that are the concern of the Maiden Goddess (independence, identity, first loves, etc.). At the peak of the full moon, it is the time of the Mother. During this period of time, we focus our ritual work in deepening our relationship with a Mother Goddess and we might elect to work on issues associated with motherhood: birth, generation, creation, and bringing things into fruition. Finally, this variant culminates with the New Moon/Dark Moon. This is the time of the Crone. During this period of time, we honor the Crone Goddesses, the Grandmothers of our faith. We engage in work that deepens our understanding of issues of loss, change, adaptation, wisdom, and magic. It is a time to engage in rituals that facilitate clearing the way for new growth, healing from grief, and contemplating what we need to let go and perhaps who we need to forgive.

Variant 2

In this cycle, the lunar month is broken into four components, rather than three. These components are as follows:

- ☽ the waxing crescent, Maiden;
- ☽ the full moon, Mother;
- ☽ the waning crescent, Crone; and
- ☽ the new moon, Death/Silence.

In this structure, the Crone becomes an object of worship and connection and is still reflective of light, thus the bringer of wisdom and hope through darkness. The Crone reflects vitality, rather than diminishment. In the New Moon we are confronted with death, silence, aloneness and how we must wrestle with the dark moments when we feel entirely bereft and alone—this is the Nothingness, the place from which Eurynome was born. As such, when the moon once more begins to build, we too may be literally reborn in the vital energy of the Maiden. I personally value this variant more than the threefold version as I feel it fosters a more valuable vision of age that shows it not as synonymous with death, but as a source of a new kind of vitality. The Mother does not give birth only to attend to death, rather with the loss of fertility, comes a new kind of fertility—that of self-creation, self-initiation. Think about how many new starts many of our older citizens have launched into after their years of parenting are complete. In this capacity, the waning crescent, like the waxing before, echoes the possibility of the new. At the same time this fourfold cycle reminds us that we all must encounter a moment of existential aloneness. Like Persephone and Ishtar, we must each descend into the depths of the cave where we are for a time utterly naked, exposed and alone, until we too find passage back into a renewed life. In this fashion, the New Moon may be best honored through a period of solitary silence or contemplation.

Selecting a Lunar Cycle as your dominant cycle of the year is one of nighttime. If you are someone who finds they work best at night, enjoys the dark, and feels more intuitive and psychic during this period of time, then a Lunar Cycle as your primary cycle of worship time can be ideal. These cycles are ideal for small, intimate groups or solitary worship and are generally more subdued. Additionally, this is a time-intensive cycle of the year, with lots of opportunity for group or solitary worship. Each month has at least three to four opportunities for religious engagement. This can be ideal if you are looking to bring more consistency and regularity into your worship life. In Wicca, moon cycles are seen as the "working"[8] rituals where magic is conducted, rather than celebration cycles; thus becoming the butter and bread of a Wiccan coven—the staple, so to speak.

Finally, the Lunar Wheel is an opportunity for a coven or group to create their own unique traditions that are intimately connected to the natural world their community is connected too. It can be a wonderful communal activity in coming together to discuss each other's lunar-month nature observations to see what shared sights seem most prominent during each moon phase. In this capacity, the group co-creates the tradition of worship and thus increases the group bonding as well as the relevance of worship for their own lives.

☽ ○ ☾

Harvest Dance

The Harvest Wheel is an agrarian-based fourfold cycle. While there are a wealth of Goddess-based harvest holidays that are culturally unique (discussed shortly in the Mythic Dance), the Harvest Cycle refers specifically to the widely agreed upon celebrations in Neopaganism. These are also known as "fire holidays" or the "cross-quarters". I prefer Harvest as this is in keeping with the agrarian aspects of these days: to bless livestock, seeding, reaping, and storing. At the same time, relabeling these as "Harvest" days also keeps central the interrelationship of these agrarian tasks (our central reliance upon the Earth to sustain us) to the sustaining nature of the Goddess as the Grain Mother, Mother Earth, Mother Nature, the Goddess of the Flowers, the Maidens of the Hunt, etc. In general the Harvest days are:

☽ February 1 or 2[9]; known as Imbolc (meaning "in the belly"), Oilmelc (meaning "ewe's milk"), and Candlemas. This was the traditional holiday that celebrated the first milks of the sheep or the beginning lactations of animals kept as livestock. It is associated with the time of growing light and thus a Maiden holiday—known as the "Festival of Waxing Light". In Goddess traditions that include this cycle, this day is seen as the day of initiation for new Goddess adherents. As such it is a time of reflection, anointing, and purification. It is a time of optimism and to begin actively putting plans in place. The traditional Goddess associated with this day is Brigid. However, Goddesses that are inherent wisdom teachers, such as Sophia, Aradia, Cerridwen are also important as this is the day when we enter into or renew our relationship with the Divine Female as our teacher and guide for the coming year. It is a time symbolized by the color white and candles.

☽ April 30/May 1, Beltaine/Beltane/May Eve. This was the traditional beginning of "test" marriages[10] in older communities and the time of planting. It is traditionally a time of growing passion and sexual energy. Maypoles (phallic symbols) and large pit fires (vaginal symbols) are visible to ensure the fertility of the people, the nonhuman animals, and the crops. In Goddess Traditions, this is a day of the burgeoning Love Goddesses, the goddesses that remind us to find our heart's desires and our passions, which in turn will bring us fruitfulness. As such, the Goddess such as Aphrodite may be invoked. Additionally because this is a coming-of-age celebration where we transition from youth to adulthood, Maiden goddesses such as Diana/Artemis may also be called upon. They represent the capacity for choice—the opportunity to choose how we will enter into adulthood. This is the counterpoint to Samhain and as such it is also held that on this day the veil between the physical and nonphysical universes is thin.

- August 2, Lughnasdh/Lammas. This is the first official harvest celebration when the grains have finally arrived after the planting of the spring. It is a time of feasting and celebrating. It is also traditionally seen as a marriage day, where vows to each other may be made and as such reflects a growing maturity, a sense of being ripened. During this time Mother Goddesses of the Grain and the Earth are focused on, such as Demeter/Ceres. Additionally, Goddesses that reflect abundance and fertility may be engaged with, such as a Habondia. In many respects this is the counterpoint day to Imbolc, whereby the light that only hinted at the possibilities to come has now matured and become fully fledged.

- October 31, Samhain/Hallowmas/"Summer's End", Hallows, All Soul's Night, Dia de los Muertos. This is one of the most popular days of celebration in most of Neopagan groups. In the Goddess traditions that follow this cycle, this is seen as the end of the year and the beginning of the "Dreaming Time". It is the time of the Crone Goddess, when the world's lushness is waning. When Demeter begins to mourn her daughter's time in the underworld and allows the earth to lie fallow. It reminds us that we best make preparations for the coming winter and that in life there are times when we must let things lie fallow, we must let things die, and we must let go. In this fashion, during this holiday we look to connecting with the Crone Goddesses, the grandmothers or in many witchcraft traditions Hecate[11]. It is a time when the veil between the living and the dead is thin and thus marks a day of ancestor worship. It is a time of divination, dreaming, and introspection—when we prepare ourselves to enter a period or restfulness, clarification, and aloneness. Dianic High Priestess, Ruth Barrett, often encourages during this period of time opportunities to sit in the dark and alone—to mirror that of the Goddess's journey into the underworld, into the depths, into the dark night of the soul.

If you select the Harvest Wheel alone, then your ritual year's purpose is most broadly on the role of balancing sustenance as we relate to the world around us. Remember the Harvest wheel emerged based on our ancestor's growing relationship on how to till the soil and how to breed animals for livestock; thus it relates to how we have internalized the goddess powers. As such it is a year's cycle that is personal, focused on how and what we seed, birth, grow, and pass followed once more by return of these cycles. It is about our capacity to cross through the veils, to divine the future, and to be conduits for the Goddess. It is a time to reflect on *our* role as priest/esses of the Goddess in our lives and how we live our lives in keeping with her values and rhythms. This is the dance of the "thou art Goddess".

❁

☽ ○ ☾

Something to consider about the Harvest Wheel: in a time of ecological crisis and a reexamination of the human impact upon the nonhuman world, the Harvest Wheel and its sources of inspiration deserves a second look. In many traditions this wheel is takes priority over the innate cycles in the natural world (such as the Lunar and Solar Wheels). With this wheel as the primary emphasis, it locates human beings above nonhuman life and emphasizes power-over relationships (hierarchical and paternalistic) through the emphasis on the capacity of humans to manage and shape the nonhuman environment. The implication of this wheel is it thealogically risks idealizing behaviors that are foundational in the emergence of the human exemptionalist belief (i.e. humans are outside of the processes of Nature, we can control the circumstances of our lives both locally and internally and at the level of Nature)[12]; thus ultimately supporting the separation between human and divinity. Agrarian behavior (while it has allowed us as a species to survive, thrive, and rapidly reproduce) also marked the beginnings of the decay of nature and the rise of deforestation and extinction; the submission of other species as "less than" and allocated to "food" status; the rise of the city and the co-occurring oppression of other humans; and the eventual creation of much of our problematic technology. In short, it began the long spiral downward from a view of the world as wholly (holy) sacred to the sanctification of the human being as the destined pinnacle of power and the elevation of our capacity to manage the environment as representative of our divine gifts.

As the Goddess is ultimately intertwined with the nonhuman world, whereby the Earth itself is Her, it is critical that thealogians engage in debate about the prominence of the agrarian holidays and what their implications are (both beneficially and nonbeneficially) within the current ecological crisis faced worldwide. In this capacity, thealogians need to be mindful of anthropocentrism or humancentrism[13] within their own thealogical frameworks. This mindfulness may also lead to new ways of envisioning this wheel in such as way as to be ecologically mindful or ecologically redemptive in quality. As such, I encourage theologians to experiment with revisioning the meanings of the Harvest Wheel within an ecocentric and ecofeminist perspective.

Solar Dance

The **Solar Wheel** comprises the four cardinal days that are typically added to the Harvest Wheel to create the eight-fold calendar year common in most Celtic and Wicca traditions (in the Developmental Dance section we'll look at how these eight holidays flow together in a whole dance). The Solar Wheel is based entirely on the visible relationship between the Earth and the Sun as manifested by light—equal days of light and lowest and highest light. In a broad way this cycle is literally all about the turning of a natural wheel (similar to the Wheel tarot card), whereby we find ourselves throughout our lives and in our years on the upside of things, the height of our year and goodness, and we find ourselves at times at the low point. This wheel also evokes a consciousness that we are not always in control—our lives are impacted by processes outside ourselves, sometimes divine and sometimes related to those who share our lives with us. At the same time, this wheel also reminds us that there are constants in our lives—while change is always occurring, we can know the sun will rise and that the earth will spin and cycle around the sun.

During the course of the year, we often strive to find a balance, to stay on even keel emotionally, physically, and culturally. Those times are best reflected in the balanced light cycles. For every reversal of fortune, we will eventually seek a way to tip the scales back up toward a sense of stability. In Nature, the Solar Wheel, is the Goddess's capacity to strike balance—to ensure that Nature flourishes and is constrained. There is always balance. The Solar Wheel Cycle is manifested by the following days[14]:

☽ ○ ☾

☽ December 20-23, Winter Solstice/Yule—this often marks the beginning of the New Year, while Samhain marks the ending. Here we are at the point of lowest light, the reversal of the wheel, and things can only get better from here. During Yule we celebrate the coming of light and the upturning of the wheel once more. In Scandinavia, well-wishers say "*got jule*", meaning "Good Wheel"—a blessing for a positive year to come. We look ahead with optimism and begin to make new plans. We must rise up and resurrect ourselves anew. In mythic tradition this is the time of Cybele, Mary, Inanna, and Isis. The Divine Mothers and Lovers who oversee or literally seek out to resurrect their sons and lovers to bring new hope and new light to the world—the literal return of the promise of fertility.

☽ March 20-23, Spring Equinox/Ostara and September 20-23, Fall Equinox/Mabon. In most Goddess traditions, the Fall and Spring Equinox are based on the grounding myth of Persephone/Kore. A critical myth in the goddess traditions. Kore is the spring aspect, the maiden child returned anew to her Mother, where the world celebrates her resurrection from the land of the dead. It is the only myth whereby the resurrecting child is a girl, rather than a male deity. In the Fall, marks the time where Kore transforms into the Wife/Lover and descends into the underworld as Persephone, and the upper world mourns her loss. In this fashion, the Fall and Spring equinox reflect balance (birth and death; creation and constraint). During the Spring celebration it is the time of anticipating the harvest and welcoming the seed back to the soil. It is a time of encouraging the Earth anew and for growth. Goddesses of this time or those that represent Mother Earth, such as Kore's mother Ceres, or the Germanic Eostre/Ostre ("estrus" meaning to be fertile). It is a time of welcoming fertility and thus symbols of eggs and rabbits are found as the whole of Nature becomes rejuvenated. During

> the Fall it is the Harvest of the "First Fruits"—of gathering them before they rot on the ground—thus not missing opportunities but biting into the last juicy bits of life before things die. It is the time of "Thanksgiving," of sharing our gratefulness to those in our lives. It is a time of saying what needs to be said and ensuring that we have not taken anything for granted.

Selecting the Solar Wheel for yourself or your community focuses on the big pictures of Nature and your relationship in Nature. It looks at how you are contained within the broad cycles of Nature and subject to growth and constraint. You, like all your fellow living brethren, must grow in comfort with the cycles of light and darkness, of abundance and paucity. It is a cycle that emphasizes living fully and honestly in the moment and in synch with the rhythm of the Great Mother. Immanence is not emphasized in this cycle, rather it is eminence—that is the Goddess, the triple Fates, the Mother-Keepers of Time who guide your life and come to the forefront. It is a time of literally going with the flow. You may find that selecting this cycle to focus on is necessary, simply because you struggle with remaining in the moment or struggle with coping with pessimism and dealing with negative events in your life that are outside of your control. This is the time of letting go and literally letting Goddess aid in your year.

Seasonal Dance

The **Seasonal Wheel** has three variants depending on which one is most resonant with you. The meaning behind the seasonal wheel is similar to that of the Solar one, with only some minor differences.

Variant 1: Threefold Year

The first variant in the Seasonal Wheel is one that divides the year into three broad seasons: Spring, Summer, and Winter. Each of these seasons corresponds to the personified aspect of the Great Goddess: Maiden, Mother, and Crone. When marking the seasonal year, generally a celebration would occur every four months:

- ☽ May would mark the Spring and thus the Maiden Goddess;
- ☽ September would mark the Summer, and thus the Mother Goddess; and
- ☽ January the Winter and thus mark the Crone.

The days you select for these celebrations may be days that ancient societies held public rituals for a goddess, for example celebrating the Goddess Maia on May 1st; the Goddess Radha on September 1st; and Gamelia or Anna Perenna on January 1st. Optionally, you may also select your three most personal Goddess patrons and craft your own ritual calendar.

Variant 2: The Fourfold Year

The Fourfold Year is very similar to the Solar Calendar, except it follows the four seasons Spring, Summer, Autumn, and Winter rather than light cycles. Remember defining the beginnings of Summer and Winter, Fall and Spring based on the solar dates is a relatively new phenomena. In antiquity, the seasons were determined based on the temperature, vegetation, weather, and the behavior wildlife. As such determining the days when the seasons change requires some observation in your area and, like the Lunar Wheel, I generally recommend taking a year to observe your specific environment to determine the time when seasons shift. Optionally, for simplicity's purpose, you can additionally follow the dates noted in the Solar Wheel. The fourfold seasonal cycle follows Spring = Maiden; Summer = Mother; Fall = Crone; and Winter = the act of cycle of Death and Rebirth.

Variant 3: The Five-Fold Celtic Year

☽ ○ ☾

This is a cycle of time where the year follows the birth, growth, passion, aging, death, and rebirth cycle of the Goddess and her Child. In the Five-Fold year, Spring is related to Growth and the Maiden; Summer is related to Passion and the Mother; Fall is related to Aging and the Crone; followed by Early Winter marking Death; and the final days of Winter symbolizes the Birth of the Divine Child. Depending on your choices the day of Death ranges from Samhain to a date around the time of Yule, with the Birth of the Divine child occurring in January through February.

❀

Seasonal Wheels can be rich ways of developing a spiritual wheel that is intimately linked to the ecological environment and rhythm of Nature. This wheel can provide a rich path for merging a spiritual framework with a consciousness of the current environmental crisis and exploring the range of spirituality as a means to address and redress environmental challenges. Additionally, this wheel can serve to ground your year within the rich material of the faces of the Goddess and allow you to explore all Her aspects and how they manifest externally in your life as well as how you manifest those elements. It allows for the thealogical conception that the Goddess is complete unto herself and cannot be divided. That She is whole and all aspects and subsequent myths are reflections of Her personality, so to speak. In this capacity, the Seasonal Wheel emphasizes thealogical wholeness and unity, while at the same time encouraging self-exploration (one's immanence) and the presence of the full Goddess in Her eminence (as she surrounds and manifests within the world around you).

Mythic Dance

Throughout our human history, the Goddess has been worshipped worldwide in many of her thousands of aspects. We still have information and records on when Her holidays were celebrated and I call this the **Mythic Wheel**—although perhaps better may be the "historical dance". If you have particularly patron Goddesses you feel very close to than your year of worship may simply be based on the days ancestors dedicated to these deities. Research into historical festivals can also provide you not only with the approximate date of worship, but ideas to create a modern ceremony in keeping with the past energy.

Developmental Dance

The **Developmental Wheel** follows the eightfold cycle, drawing together the Solar and Harvest wheels. Because the Goddess traditions are gener-

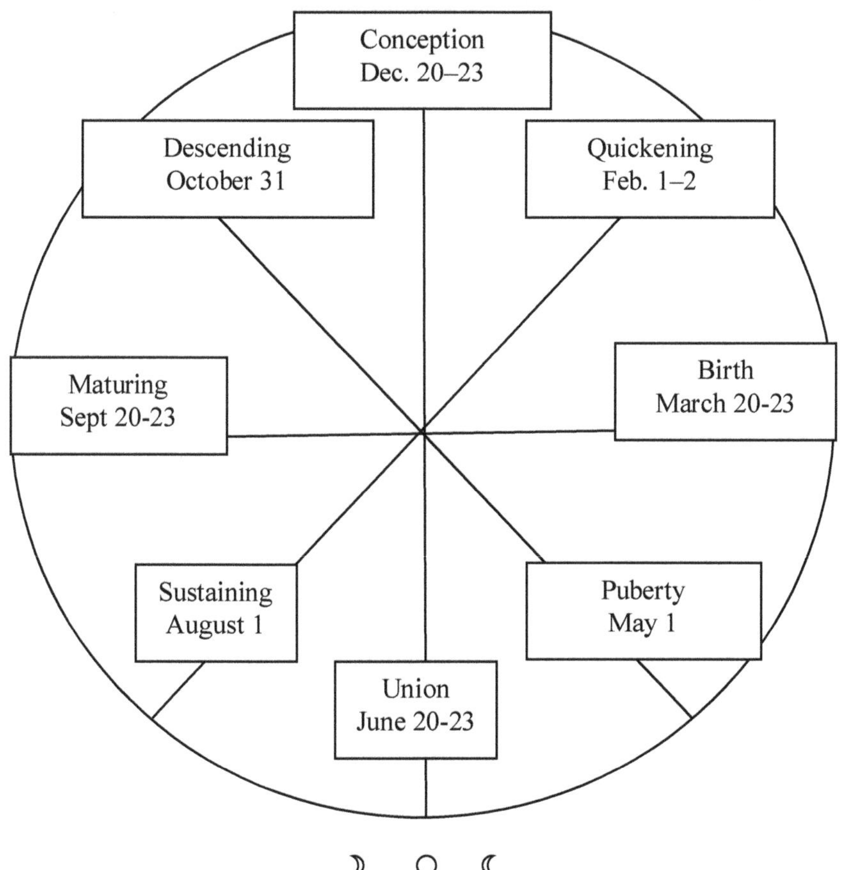

ally geared toward women alone[15], the developmental wheel generally speaks to the development of women. However, I will be noting how men, too, can participate equally and fully in this cycle as well to encourage the actually equality of the genders rather than maintain any notion that one gender is more right than another. The wheel is the Developmental Wheel. It follows the eightfold wheel of the year, only its focus is on the mythic developmental journey of the Goddess and the developmental journey of our lives. There are two ways through which this wheel can inform our ritual structures. First we may look at it as a yearly cycle (more on this in a moment) or we can look at it as the broad communal cycles for those who are members of our ministry. Thus it becomes a cycle of Life proper, rather than a cycle contained in one year. Let's look at these cycles from both perspectives.

When we look at the above wheel we can see how each of us in our lives passes through this dance. We are conceived, born, become sexually mature, join with another, we mature, and we die. In this capacity, we find how Goddess traditions value and celebrate the eight cycles of life:

☽ Conception—many rituals within the Goddess tradition, as well as in many Neopagan traditions look toward increasing fertility and encouraging conception. In the life cycle, we work to help and celebrate those who are seeking to have children; while at the same time ensuring that we do not dislocate those who opt not to have children from their important role in life. It is ideal to craft rituals and ceremonies for those who choose not to have children, for in Nature these individuals serve to ensure that there remain enough resources for the whole. We find evidence of many species choosing not to procreate and through their sacrifice they ensure the lives of those who do. As such when we consider celebrating conception or providing women or couples with ritual power to conceive, it is important we equally honor those who do not. It is also important to include men in this process who may be connected to your ritual community. We often dislocate men from the child-birthing process and this serves to increase men's psychological distance from their children and their role as "Father". Finally, conception may also be understood as the process of creating one's purpose (and subsequently moving through a birthing process to bring this into fruition—this is also particularly important for women who often are unable to consider their purpose in a society that often limits their viable roles).

☽ Pregnancy (quickening)—we craft blessing rituals for our sisters who are pregnant to ensure a safe experience. We encourage them to bond with their unborn infant and facilitate the spiritual context of these powerful moments. We seek out the opportunities to hear about their experiences as they become intimately one with a new life and thus a living voice of the Goddess as She birthed Herself and us into the world. We also use this time to encourage any fathers who are present to feel an intimate part of nature, like the serpent Ophion, who sheltered and nurtured the cosmic egg before birth, like the sea horse or the male Emperor penguin who shepherds the growing seed into life. We also encourage the community to protect the growing life, just as the sister wolves of a pack bring food and support to the nest-building mother.

☽ Birth, like all religions worldwide, we celebrate the birth of infants. In the Goddess tradition, it is customary to give 13 blessings to the child to carry them through life. Birth is a communal affair as we welcome each child into the world. Each child is a sacred manifestation of the Goddess and a moment for us to reflect upon the sheer wonder of how life emerges.

☽ Puberty (the development of secondary sexual characteristics, often between 10 and 15 years of age in boys and girls).

Worldwide, there have been long traditions welcoming our youth into adulthood and celebrating their coming of age as fertile (literally "creative" beings). In our modern society, we have lost the benefit of sustaining and meaningful rituals at this stage and most of our youth self-initiate with sometimes disastrous consequences (teen pregnancy, addition, crime). Our girls of our society often feel the need to deny their womanhood in favor of starving themselves to the point of boyishness or waifishness. They develop unhealthy images of their bodies and are often profoundly sexually victimized. Our boys in turn do not develop a healthy view of women or a deep view of themselves as emotional and compassionate beings. We throw our youths into the maze of adulthood as a "trial by fire" and hope they come out somewhat okay in the end. In Goddess traditions, and in most Neopagan traditions, this is a time of guidance of our youth and celebrating their value to the community. It is a time of supporting them and showing them their power and how to use it. It is a time of shepherding the next generation into an adulthood that is joyous and responsible, respectful and proud.

☽ Union. In Neopagan traditions there is a strong emphasis to steer away from heterosexist language that precludes the love relationships of Gay, Lesbian, and Transgendered men and women, as such we refer to this stage as "union" rather than marriage. Further this encompasses a wide range of meaningful types of unions we experience in our lives as well. In this fashion, union reflects the moment(s) we decide to join with another person, to forgo our sense of "oneness" for a shared purpose with another. We celebrate this joining as the opportunity to manifest and sustain the world. Together we are stronger and more capable than alone. We can better provide for those around us and we can experience the deep connect that the Web of Life promises. We become at once Eurynome and the

North Wind. In ritual life this is typically known as handfasting.

- Sustaining. We often don't think of crafting rituals for the process of how we spend most of our adulthoods—in the activity of sustaining our lives and those who depend on us. We often don't think of celebrating our ingenuity, our sacrifices, and our inventiveness that supports our lives and those around us. Nevertheless, the Goddess encourages us to wonder at and celebrate our capacity to sustain: our capacity to meet our needs—our self-reliance; our capacity to meet challenges that require creative problem-solving. Rituals here are all about how we get through the challenging moments in life and honoring ourselves and each other.

- Maturation (menopause in men[16] and women). This is also known as the ceremony of Croning (women) or Saging (men). In the Goddess wheel and Neopaganism in general, we honor and celebrate our elders. We celebrate the time when individuals come of age again. When they transition into the Crone Goddess or the Sage God. We respect and seek out their wisdom; we acknowledge and celebrate the whole of their life and encourage them to live juicily (after all this occurs during the First Fruits celebration) in the twilight of their lives. We acknowledge of the richness and joyfulness that is still awaiting them as they transition into Cronehood/Sagehood.

- Descent (dying and death). As with all religious paths, we come to the comfort of the dying and the grieved and ensure the safe passage of the Dead in funeral rites. In the Goddess paths, death is simply a passage to rebirth. It is the descent of Persephone into her other life. It is the downward spiral of the wheel, which will soon turn upward again, as we welcome in new members to our Earthly lives, while honoring those who have passed on.

☽ ○ ☾

When we look at this cycle as a year cycle, we look at how we interact with our personal goals and ideas and creativity. Instead of conception of new life, we look at the conception of new ideas and changes. Instead of looking at quickening, we look at the process of gestating on our goals and ideas—the process of thinking about what it is we hope to achieve in the year. In Birth, we look at putting plans into motion—getting our ideas out there and the changes made. In Puberty, we focus our attention on nurturing what is delicate within us, what is newly born, what is getting ready to transition away from us. During union, we might assess our relationship to others and our ideas, how can we honor our intimate connections or increase our opportunities for deeper relationships in the year. In sustaining, we look at what sustains us and how we have sustained others or our goals during the year thus far. We take stock on what resources we still need. During maturation, we look at what growth we have made during the year to be honored—what wisdom was achieved. When we reach the phase of dying and death, we look at what we must relinquish; what aspects of our year must we let go of, what goodbyes need to be made to create room for the rebirth of the new year.

☽ ○ ☾

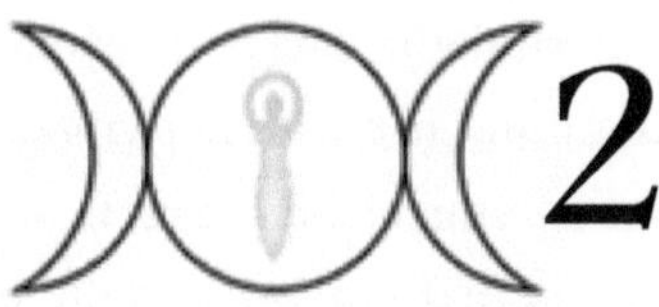

VIRGIN! She who is sufficient unto Herself.
—Donna Wilshire

The Solar Maiden

Defining the Virgin–Maiden

> For early cultures the word "virgin" did not mean "one who has never had sex." For a female it meant one who is neither the dependent child nor wife of a man, but rather one who belongs to herself.[1]

One of the primary misconceptions many individuals coming to know the Goddess have is what the term maiden and virgin mean with respect to the youngest aspect of the triple goddess. In antiquity the term virgin was not synonymous with sexual chastity, but rather reflected singleness. As Donna Wilshire notes the virginal goddess is self-contained; her primary focus is on manifesting her specific skills and growing within the world. She is not a life-giver as she is a life-enhancer (although some myths also reflect her capacity to give birth). The myths of the Virgin–Maiden goddesses demonstrate that she is a figure who is approached by adherents to aid them in specific facets of their life—whether it relates to a type of nonhuman animal species they require for sustenance, building their warrior skills, or meting out justice.

In the Virgin–Maiden we have two specific aspects, her Bright–Solar Self and her Dark–Lunar Self. In her Bright Self she is a warrior, the intellect, optimism and sunlight. She is a comforter and provider. She beautifies the world around her with her vibrancy and fertility of youth and potentiality. She is ethical and direct. She is reliable and ever-returning, reminding us that our own youth, enthusiasm, capacity for renewal and discovery is ever present, not something we have grown out of.

In Her Dark aspect, she is watery, flexible, and wild. She sees what cannot be seen in the bright sunlight. She is sexual. She is swift and profound in her judgment. She is mystical and intuitive. She anticipates her Crone aspect in her capacity for magic, shape-shifting, and transformation. She is elusive—just when we feel and think we have fully understood her, she slips away, changing her appearance. She challenges our own certainty—reminding us to be flexible, to go further, and to trust in our intuitive selves. She reminds us to dive below our rational selves, for in her youth she has yet to become rooted to social expectations and ways of knowing. The Dark Maiden is instinctive and trusts her own sense of the deeper truths under the surface.

In all her aspects, she is complete unto herself. The Virgin–Maiden has unclouded vision. She has no need for definition through companionship. Her own creative actions speak for themselves. She is focused on making her own unique presence known in the universe. She symbolizes the unleashing of energy in the universe. As such when we connect with her, we are finding a path to our own completeness. We are reengaging with a vital spark of energy of youth—the excitement of seeing the world anew. We are coming to recognize that we, alone, are essential to the flowing of life and that we may always find again our innate gifts.

A Year of the Bright, Solar Maiden

While tradition holds the year is a cycle of the Goddess as she grows from Maiden to Mother to Crone, we can also celebrate the solar year in her Virgin–Maiden aspect alone. Why might we do this? First, we may

☽○☾ **Symbol & Ritual Tip**

While we often interpret the symbolic meanings of the Virgin–Maiden within the framework of our own spiritual and psychological needs. We can deepen our understanding of her when we consider her as not one who enables our own growth, but whose presence and beingness may guide us in living more holistically within the web of life. Arcane myths are decidedly humancentric; however in the contemporary era we have become increasingly aware of our interconnections to life. As such rediscovering the thealogical possibilities of the Virgin–Maiden as embodying an environmental ethic can provide a deeper and richer foundation for our own spiritual lives. For example, we might explore Aphrodite's "green thumb"[2] whereby her transition from shore to land, brought about a rejuvenation and revivification of the wildspaces into fertile spring. She is the ripening force that ensures the wilds of the world remain fertile and bountiful—in short we might consider her as a countering the widespread human behaviors that lead to extinction. Further, as a Goddess born of the sea, the ocean and the life within is sacred to her and thus reminds us that our own care of the ocean is essential in our honoring of this being. As we re-examine the myths of the Goddesses from around the world, we can develop rituals that encourage us to actively engage in the care of the non-encultured worlds and to expand our sense of self to become, like the Goddess Herself, inclusive of all living beings.

feel personally called to the Solar Virgin–Maiden aspect because our lives most closely resonate with her diverse Solar aspects. The Solar Virgin–Maiden is not without developmental growth—as we will see, a year in her cycle shows her own growth and transformation.

She, like all of us is not simply born and in a brief period suddenly disappears into parent- and partner- hood. Rather exploring the year of the Solar Virgin–Maiden, we find that she begins with exploring her

☽ ○ ☾

own creative potential and capacity to demonstrate and master her innate skills. She moves to exploring her sexuality. She develops compassion and grows into a nurturer. She grows in intellect and unclouded wisdom; and she faces loss and learns to comfort her grief. In this fashion, if you are still in your years of aloneness and independence or you have returned to a state independence and are looking to increase your own vitality, optimism, creative potential, and reawaken your gifts to deploy perhaps into a new work role than a year with the Solar Virgin–Maidens is ideal.

Before we dive into our year, a Solar Virgin–Maiden year differs somewhat from traditional Neopagan views where by the new year begins at Samhain. In a Solar Virgin–Maiden year, the year developmentally must begin at Yule and end at Samhain, where our Solar Virgin–Maiden must face a transition and transformation—where light inevitably gives way to lesser light.

Something to Consider

When you begin to craft a Solar Virgin–Maiden year it can be beneficial to spend some time journaling about your own experiences as a Virgin–Maiden. What were your emotional themes and developmental changes? What were your concerns and focuses—when did you experience high and low energy? Where did you experience maturity and insight into your cycles and were there any "unfinished" aspects of your own Maiden–Virgin growth? You may wish to consider exploring what elements would be the domain of the Solar and the Lunar Maiden–Virgins to refine your list. These questions allow you to consider your own personal cycles or rather how you will likely experience Solar Virgin–Maiden energy within a year dedicated to her being and your own rejuvenation. Once you've done this, you can begin to explore the myths and rites of the Solar Virgin–Maidens that will most likely resonate with your own energy throughout the year. Further, this will personalize the meanings of each sacred day within the year in such a way as to increase

☽ ○ ☾

their potency and impact in your own life. Thus you craft a thealogy that is applicable to day-to-day life. If you work with a group of women have all members share their developmental experiences to look for common themes to craft a year that resonates with the group.

A Solar Maiden–Virgin Story of Yule

(December 21–23, Western Hemisphere)

At Yule, the Cosmic Mother is ready to give birth to herself once more. She has been gestating since October and, in the longest night of the year, has begun to experience labor pains. We have kept vigil at the impending birth; we have literally become Doulas to the Mother. Our vigil is ruled by peace and joyfulness, just as the Maiden Goddess Eirene stands with us. She reminds us that to welcome the new child, we must create a space of love and peace. We must set aside our anxieties and frustrations and be peaceful within us. The Birthing-Mother should not be focused on keeping us calm—she has too much work to do. And so we prepare for the coming Divine Solar Maiden–Virgin child by keeping the hearth lit and the lights on. Our home is warm and welcoming. We are filled with peace and give the gifts of peace to those around us. We are filled with optimism, excitement, and hope. And in our celebrating we demonstrate to the Great Mother that this is a world where her daughter will be honored.

And finally, at sunrise, her child, the Mother Goddess Birthing Herself, has returned to the Earth. And so the Dawn is born. She is the beautiful Eos, Thesan, Ushas, and Aurora. She brings the wisdom of the certainty of new beginnings, fresh starts, and optimism to grow and shine on one's life. She is the Goddess Who Reaches. She embraces life and all its possibilities, ever-seeking a better view of all that is. She sparkles in the light, radiating a rich rainbow of oranges, reds, and yellows. Yet her radiance does not blind those who look to see her—her heat does not burn. She is approachable and encouraging. Each morning she weeps in

☽○☾ **Symbol & Ritual Tip**

There are a wide range of mythological and deity possibilities for inclusion in a Yule/Winter Solstice ritual—and this also includes reworking patriarchal myths—myths for example where the "birth" process is co-opted by male deities, such as Athena. Additionally, you can re-imagine, create, or explore the elusive birth stories of Solar Maiden–Virgin Goddesses to identify symbols and ritual ideas to celebrate her birth. Another question worth exploring is how the goddess Maiden–Virgins are born fully empowered, whereas birth stories of male deities typically require their consumption of another deity (over the mother) or an act of aggression to prove their worth in order to obtain their adult and complete status. Goddesses are born complete.

joy at the beauty of the world and her tears become the dew that nourishes life. She rises heavenward on the wings of the White Heron who feeds in the rushes in the earliest hours of day. She rises with the thrill of being alive.

And in her birth and rise into the sky, she frees herself from her Mother's womb. As the Goddess Libertas, she cuts her own umbilicus to rise independent—no longer does she need nourishment form another, for she is complete in herself. And in the Dawn, the Maiden–Virgin becomes freed from the dark of the womb to fully manifest herself.

Solar Maiden–Virgin Mystery Rite for Yule

During the Solar Maiden–Virgin Yule, you become a Doula, a sacred supporter of the Great Mother's birth. You are the companion to the Goddess and her rebirth into the world. This is a time of creating an environment that is peaceful, joyous, and alive to the senses. Consider scenting your home with spices of apple, frankincense, pine, and evergreen. Hang mistletoe, ivy and holly; all of which remind us of the constancy of life and the ever-presence of the Goddess. In particular, the Mistletoe reflects the coming virginal Daughter-Goddess, who has yet to pass through her menses. While Holly reminds us of the Mother's blood—the berry of fertility that allows for birth and rebirth with a white blossom always a reminder that the Mother gives birth to herself and retains her Virginal aspect within her. And Ivy to reflect the warrior women–priestesses who defend and protect the Goddess to ensure her rebirth is safe.

Light a Yule Log and let it burn through the night to provide warmth and remind all present of the importance of having a center filled with light. The sacred log (or substitute a candle placed in a central area) encourages us to focus on what grounds and centers us and where our hearts are. Dedicate a living Yule tree to the Mother that will be planted (or is already planted preferably) in honor of her daughter. Decorate it with family and friends as the Dawn will soon be dressed up by the raiment of the sky. Consider having you and your guests make ornaments by hollowing out eggs and painting them with your hopes, aspirations, and your innate talents you wish to birth in the coming year.

Have a communal feast and give blessings of peace to each member at the table and say a prayer of peace for the world that the world returns to light and love and that the whole of the environment once more is renewed. Give thanks to the Mother who is transitioning into the Daughter and all the renewed life that she will now bring to the world. Conclude with giving meaningful gifts that support the unique aspects of each guest—gifts that reflect an understanding of who that individual is unto themselves. And before your celebration is over, create and tell a story of the Divine Maiden's birth to anticipate her arrival.

Wake up at Dawn the next day and leave an offering for the birds of the wild who are the friends of the Dawn Maiden–Virgin. Welcome her back into the world. Consider cutting your own umbilicus that has you tied to something unhealthy in your life or something that you no longer need to be dependent upon—liberating yourself from your own darkness as you welcome in the dawn.

☽ ○ ☾

A Solar Maiden–Virgin Story of Imbolc

(February 1 or 2, Western Hemisphere)

As the months pass since Yule, the Maiden–Virgin grows in strength and brightness. She is maturing from divine child to adolescent. She reaches the moment of her first blood—she becomes fertile unto herself. Her potentiality for creativity has rapidly expounded. At any moment she can transform herself into a Mother should she feel the time is right and that she has accomplished all she has set to do. Yet she won't do this just yet. Her focus is on committing Herself to Herself—of embracing her uniqueness and discovering her vision of the world. This is a time of initiation and coming into the recognition of her own creative potential. And the Child-Goddess transforms into Brigit and Athena.

This is the time of the Mind—the experiencing of her brilliance. This is the time of her capacity to create with her words and her intellect and her hands. She discovers her skills and talents and expresses this. As Brigit, She is the creative potential manifest—she is a Divine Poet and comes to fully understand the power of her hands and her ability to initiate action. As Athena she discovers her keen ability to strategize and plan—to consider consequences and find creative solutions to problems. She discovers her capacity to root herself and stand firm for her beliefs. She manifests all facets of intelligence: creative, emotional, rational/intellectual, and physical prowess. She fully embodies her being and celebrates the fullness of her being. She is all at once the Intellect and the Heart.

Solar Maiden–Virgin Mystery Rite for Imbolc

During the Maiden–Virgin Imbolc we are asked to commit ourselves to ourselves and our innate talents. This is a time when we can honor and celebrate that which is unique to us: our talent and creative vision, our intellect and way of seeing the world, our beliefs and values—what we

☽○☾ Symbol & Ritual Tip

Goddesses have long been associated with intellect, artistic creativity and other modes of self expression. They are the muses and sources of inspiration, they are the creators of music and poetry; they are the masters of symmetry and mind. While society traditionally allocates women into the lone creative process of motherhood, the diversity of creative power of the Goddesses is profound. At Imbolc, we can discover (and rediscover) these myths and reexamine how they may emerge within our own lives—how we, as women may become more complete creatures who create with all their capacities, rather than become confined by cultural norms to direct this energy into one element. This frees women up who cannot have children or choose not to as well as women whose children are grown and are looking for new paths to direct their creative impulses.

fight for and will stand firm for. This is a time when we embrace the Creative potential of Brigit and the Intellectual capacity of Athena. This is a time when we are empowered and assert who we are in the world and make a commitment to be authentic.

If you celebrate in a group, Imbolc is a day when you welcome the new members and their unique beings into your coven/grove—while they in turn commit their authentic spiritual selves to the group. If you celebrate with your family, this is a time to encourage each other's unique expressions and talents—perhaps it is a time to support that seemingly whimsical or risky creative dream or to find a way to solidify an individual's intellectual confidence. If you are celebrating alone, this is a time of relinquishing your doubts and embracing the energy of Brigit and Athena (or other Goddess). It is a time of stripping away all the negative messages that you may have absorbed all your life about what you can and cannot do and exploring what you want to do and who you really want to be and taking that first step to commit yourself to that core person. It is about becoming pure once more—becoming the

Virgin Goddess who is complete in herself. This is a time of knowing what's in your core—your deep belly—what you were gifted with by the Goddess at your own birth and what your Faery Godmothers or the Norns have blessed you with.

This is a reflective celebration—a time of lighting candles in recognition of the growing light and the optimism of the coming spring—when the Maiden–Virgin will manifest her creative potential. This is a time where we dress in white to reflect the purity and potential of the Maiden –Virgin. It can be a wonderful exercise for you and those you celebrate with to have a piece of white canvas set before you and to contemplate all the possibilities that may be painted on this canvas.

To receive a blessing from Brigit, place a white cloth outdoors overnight to allow her Dew to drench it. Set up an altar in your house and have your daughters (and sons!) create corn dolls in honor of Brigit and set them upon a bed in your house to encourage the blessings of Brigit for your children so that they grow into who they innately are, rather than who others think they should be. If you do not have children or your children/ grandchildren are grown create your own doll to encourage your own authenticity. To your altar add an image or carving of an owl and snake to honor Athena and to welcome your own wisdom and power. Conclude your celebrations with a dinner by candlelight where you spin a tale of Brigit and Athena.

A Solar Maiden–Virgin Story of Ostara

(March 21 or 23, Western Hemisphere)

Our Solar Maiden–Virgin Goddess has now become a young woman and seeks to manifest her creative potential. She has moved through a period of self-discovery and unlocked her intellectual, physical, and creative power. She is now ready to express these impulses—to manifest her very being in the world. She is ready to transition from the winter of internally directed energy and gestation to the spring of lushness and expres-

☽ ○ ☾

☽○☾ **Symbol & Ritual Tip**

Ostara is a rich time to celebrate the arrival of spring and to craft a Solar Maiden-Virgin ritual in commitment to protecting the Earth and its diverse species. The domain of many solar and lunar, for that matter, Maiden–Virgins is traditionally to ensure the revivification of the Earth itself. In many ways, continuing the work of the Great Mother (and her mother before her). Maiden–Virgins reflect the spirit of and possibility of evolution and adaptation within the nonhuman world (and in all respects are the sources of inspiration for our own tool and artistic development). As both adherents of the Goddess and also conduits of her powers, it's important that we also develop a healthy and balanced relationship with the nonhuman world and participate actively in the revivification of it. Some rituals that are ideal include cleanups of waterways and beaches or parks; facilitating adoption events or participating with local human societies; becoming engaged with local conservancy programs; or raising funds to support an environmental cause.

sion. She is Amaterasu, Kore, Aphrodite, and Flora. She is Spring personified with all the vitality and creativity manifesting from her hands. She has come out of her cave and the depths that flung the world into a winter and has reawakened her power to bring about the lush and diverse vibrancy of renewed life—through her the Earth becomes lush once more. All the diversity comes from her rich imagination. All the reawakened life comes from the strength of her energy. She is fascinated by her talent—she is in awe of her capabilities. She is comfortable in her aloneness for in this space she gives uninhibited rise to her own unrestrained creativity.

☽ ○ ☾

Solar Maiden–Virgin Mystery Rite for Ostara

During the Solar Maiden–Virgin Ostara life begins to renew itself. We see budding trees, the first hardy flowers, the first generation of many newborn species. Amaterasu has moved out of her cave and her self-imposed seclusion to reawaken the world and to dwell in its glory. Kore has returned from the underworld and to her singleness—a reawakened Virgin Daughter. Flora unleashes Her creative power into the vegetation of the world—strengthening the seed and encouraging the blossom.

This is a time when we express ourselves. It is a time when we take the first steps toward our personal goals. We plant the seeds of our success on this day. We seed ourselves with positive affirmations and the expectation of our success. We seed ourselves with all the tools we need to secure us in an area that will grow. We nourish ourselves with all the emotional, physical, and intellectual juices. We become rooted and ready to contribute to the landscape of diversity. We are untainted by doubt and the expectations of others—we risk the perilous journey of pushing through the egg, the cocoon, the seed. We harness the sheer will and strength that brought us from our mother's womb into this world to begin to set forth to manifest our own talents in the world.

On this day, stand in front of the mirror, just as Amaterasu did, and allow yourself to appreciate who you are. Affirm who you are in the mirror when you wake up from your cave of sleep. Appreciate your unique beauty and power as the only true way to draw you out from a protective cave of avoidance. It was only when Amaterasu saw herself in the mirror that Uzume held before her that ultimately drew her from the cave. This is not narcissism, this is truth. It is only our own selves that will draw us out from within ourselves and return us to our creative centers. As you stand in front of the mirror, say a blessing for Amaterasu's creative wisdom—She who stands between Winter and Spring.

In Kore we have another liberation story—she reminds us that even in our ties to others, we too can find time for our core creative selves—

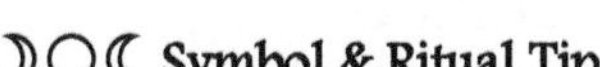

Symbol & Ritual Tip

Ostara, in the Solar Maiden–Virgin aspect, calls us to reflect upon the issue of liberation. Through many of the myths associated with the Solar Maiden–Virgins we discover themes of escape, liberation, freedom, and the transformation from a closed state to an open one. For women, this is a particularly crucial theme as many of us have experienced subtle or overt forms of oppression. Further still many women have experienced sexual or domestic violence. We may alternately opt to explore and reclaim our sense of freedom and liberate ourselves from oppressive elements of culture, whether they are internal or external in origin. Contemplating what it means to be "free" or liberated, as well as crafting a ritual in honor of or to connect to one of the liberation goddesses (such as Libertas, Feronia, Lady Godiva, Pax, Tamra, Epona) is a powerful way of celebrating Ostara.

our untouched and complete selves independent of others. If you have family responsibilities, take time away from them—assert yourself to yourself in honor of Kore. Take a cleansing bath or a crisp walk in the coming-back-to-green Earth and ask that Kore bless you.

If you celebrate with others plant bulbs and trees. Celebrate the creative ingenuity and diversity of Flore with each other. Let each person plant their own dreams and as a group commit to nourish them, just as Flora nourishes all of the new life. Consider giving baskets (symbolizing abundance) full of unique gifts that support and spark the creativity of each member in your group or family. Have a communal meal and say a blessing of success and manifestation for each participant's goals. At the end of your evening have each member tie a ribbon to a tree charged with their personal goal for manifestation.

☽ ○ ☾

A Solar Maiden–Virgin Story of Beltaine

(May 1, Western Hemisphere)

Once our Maiden–Virgin Goddess has focused her attention to manifesting her power, she begins to explore her relationship to others. She has taken time to focus on her personal goals, but now begins to see herself in relation to the wider network of others. Loneliness does not motivate her as she is complete in herself; rather curiosity and a drive for expansion and self-discovery does. In this, she begins to see how she can coexist with others without losing herself. She becomes Aparājitā, the unconquered one, capable of relating to others while remaining true to herself. In the ever-expanding vision of herself in relation to others, she becomes the Divine Messenger between us and the ether as Iris, the spring–summer rainbow. She is Tabiti—the passionate goddess of fire who merges with other species, communicating with nonhuman animals. She is Talna, awakened to her sexuality and capacity to love others, but remain wholly to herself. When we encounter this Maiden–Virgin we come to understand how we, too, can live in wholeness in our relationships to other. We learn that to be fully in a relationship with an other means to bring our authentic and complete self to this relationship—to be able to grow from it, rather than to shrink within its energy.

Solar Maiden–Virgin Mystery Rites of Beltaine

During the Maiden–Virgin Beltaine we are awakened to the expanded world around us. We no longer live within the dwellings of the mind or our inner creative drives, but seek to merge with the outer world. Yet, we are also challenged in our merging so as not to lose ourselves. The Maiden–Virgin Solar Year encounters this day of sexual awakening, celebration, and the thrall of spring is a time when our boundaries are permeable and balanced—neither too rigid nor too open. We seek out all types of relational possibilities with others and challenge ourselves to step outside our comfort zones and prejudices. We embrace the wonderful sources of learning and experience and creativity that emerge when we are our authentic selves with others as does Aparājitā. She guides us toward maintaining our dignity, self-respect, and sense of self as we engage with others. She helps us clarify what is our "stuff" and what is another's and how to reframe our relationships so that all members may retain themselves. We can purify ourselves in fire and as such, strip down to our dignified selves

As Iris, the Goddess of the Rainbow, we learn how to be a messenger of the Goddess's love as she communicates it to our Earth. We walk in grace and joyfulness. She is the epitome of diversity in her multicolored being and reminds us that through our own confident expression of our diversity in our social interactions, we too create this wondrous rainbow. We may also trust in Iris to act as the shamanic bridge between our physical world and that of the expanded universe. Taking time on this day to engage in a shamanic-like journeywork across the body of Iris, the Rainbow Bridge, we extend our relatedness more deeply into a spiritual focus. If in a group, consider designating one part of the group as the drummers—empowering you and other members to journey forward; then switch roles.

As the day of Tabiti, the fire goddess who speaks with nonhuman animals, we light the bon fires (optionally use a cauldron in your home) and contemplate the burning energy within us—our passion and strength. We place an offering of flowers to the fire and ask for Tabiti to teach us the magic of merging with nonhuman species. And thus we expand our own sense of relatedness to the wild wood. We take on the perspectives of our fellow nonhuman brethren to come to a deep appreciation for the richness of Life's diversity.

Finally, Beltaine is the day where the Maiden–Virgin Goddess discovers her sexuality and her vital sexual nature. This is a time to heal our inhibitions about sexuality and to tap into our lusty self—to feel comfortable in our bodies and with our bodies and an intimate other. In this fashion, it is also about increasing our passion for intimacy and emo-

☽○☾ Symbol & Ritual Tip

Beltaine offers us a unique opportunity to confront our own biases and stereotypes. All of us have beliefs about other people (and the nonhuman world) that would benefit from careful evaluation and purging. Our brains literally seek out short-cuts to categorize human and nonhumans alike to help us make speedier decisions when confronted (known as heuristics). The problem with these short-cuts is they typically become unconscious and are often based on the application of negative experiences (most commonly) applied to (generalized) an entire group. Beltaine is an ideal day to clean out these patterned thoughts and embrace openness and acceptance. Some places to start include issues with race, gender, religion, ablebodiness, and age—looking for any quick assumptions that might cross your mind when you encounter someone who is "other" than you. And also consider assumptions about nonhuman animals—do you have a phobia or do you think insects are "icky" while panda bears are "adorable"? Finally, consider crafting a ritual to release beliefs your family held or continues to hold about others to help create the energy of change and openness. Recognizing the value of all creatures (human and nonhuman) allows us to fully participate in the world around us and manifest the Goddess authentically—the Goddess who is the source of the unfolding diversity of all life.

tional closeness to an equal. We are no longer our Mother's children, we are our own person and seek those who are equal to us. We may ask for Talna's blessing on this day to help us engage in intimate relationships in a positive fashion with healthy attachment. We can care about the individual, but because we have a core sense of ourselves, an unconquered self, we are not threatened by the other person's capacity to change and even leave. We can be complete with and without another.

☽ ○ ☾

A Solar Maiden–Virgin Story of Litha

(June 21–23, Western Hemisphere)

The Maiden–Virgin Goddess experiences the joy and ecstasy of union with others, while still retaining a firm footing in who she is. And with this sheer enthralling and inspiring energy she arrived to Litha—having become a full Sun Goddess. She is proud and mature as she rises high above all. She remains there for the longest day—sharing her joyfulness and sense of success and Her warm ecstasy. She feels closest to the World than ever before. She is our intimate companion and stands high above us, warming us and reminding us of her devotion to herself and to us. She is Šams, the lofty South Arabian Sun Goddess, and Saules meitas, the Latvian Daughter of the Sun who grants us the gift of roses to show her devotion to us.

Solar Maiden–Virgin Mystery Rite for Litha

The Maiden–Virgin Litha is a time of fully affirming oneself to their core identity; just as the Maiden–Virgin Goddess reaffirms her identity as the Sun. She began as the Dawn at Yule during the shortest day of the year, and at the longest day of the year she assumes her full raiment as the Sun. All the time spent on honoring who she is and maintaining her unconquered self has manifested fully in her capacity to rise as the great sun, her fullest potential—overseeing the world below her. Her comfort with her singleness radiates to the world below—to us.

When we arrive at Litha it is a time of giving ourselves a pat on the back for our courage in sticking to our goals. It is a time for each of us to shine and honor our innate gloriousness. It is a time when we recommit ourselves to our authentic selves that needs no other to validate. It is a time where we honor our wholeness and to allow ourselves to feel complete. This is a day we celebrate until the Sun literally goes down.

☽ ○ ☾

☽○☾ **Symbol & Ritual Tip**

The sun, often seen as a masculine image, has a rich mythological tradition of being associated with the Goddess and there are a plethora of goddesses and their stories waiting to be told at this time of year. Women have long experienced silence—and many still do—that is comparable to the Sun Goddesses. Researching and acting out or crafting a poem or story of a Maiden–Virgin Goddess can be a powerful way to spend this day. Not only do you honor your own voice, but also actively reawaken the Voice of the Goddess.

In celebration of this day, either in group or alone, prick your finger[3] with a rose and placing a drop of blood on your forehead (self anointing) and a drop of blood on the ground, signifying your commitment to yourself and to the Maiden–Virgin Goddess. Then leave the rose in offering to the Sun, placed outside in the direct light. Adjourn to a communal meal that is filled with fresh seasonal fruits and vegetables and drink rose hips tea. Say a salutation to the Maiden–Virgin Sun Goddesses that their lights' continues to strengthen our sense of self.

A Solar Maiden–Virgin Story of Lammas

(August 1, Western Hemisphere)

The Maiden–Virgin Goddess is maturing; she has passed her zenith in the sky and is now moving toward the inevitable moment of maturity where she becomes Mother. And in this transition, she begins to experience her capacity to nurture others—to place before her those in need, those with less, those who are vulnerable. She begins to see herself as a provider—someone who is turned to because she is authentic in herself. She is honest and upfront. And because she has felt complete in herself, she is full of energy. She is the blazing sun that never ceases. She has energy to share.

☽ ○ ☾

And just as the Sun lowers in the sky, its light lessening, it is the sign that she is now giving her energy to those who reside below. She has cultivated and strengthened her energy to the degree that she can now share it directly with others. As such she becomes the Lady Habondia, Abundantia, and Nantosuelta. She is the Goddess of Abundance and Prosperity.

Solar Maiden–Virgin Mystery Rites of Lammas

The Maiden–Virgin Sun Goddess now lets loose her energy into the world, dissipating it through sharing. Her energy ripens the grains to sustain us in the time of low light—the time when she must transition. She has become so full of confidence, strength, passion, identity that she can no longer keep these gifts to herself. She reminds us to share who we are with others; to share our successes and our gifts. When we have been true to who we are, we are full of energy—we are inspired, literally—and as such we have energy to spare. We can become a fulfilling source for others and seek fulfillment in ourselves.

This is a day of being with others. Celebrating alone is insufficient to fully honor the Maiden–Virgin Goddess of Abundance. This is a day of sharing our joy, success, energy, and enthusiasm. It is a day of a communal meal where we feed those who are close to us (optionally consider engaging in work that feeds those with less). It is a day of giving a small gift to others that symbolically reflects our prayer for them to have all they need in the coming winter months. It is a day where you might wish to consider opening your house to an abandoned or young nonhuman animal. It is a time where you might consider directing your energy to a cause that is important to you or opening up your house on this day to empower a social or political cause that you feel you can contribute positively too. Energy abounds during this time as the Maiden–Virgin Goddess dissipates herself. It is a time of having that bit of extra wind to direct toward a final goal or to bring a project to completion.

☽ ○ ☾

☽○☾ Symbol & Ritual Tip

We often associate sharing our energy with others as self-sacrifice. In fact most women have been conditioned to go beyond their reserve capacities to give everything of themselves to others. This leaves us feeling drained, depressed, anxious, and angry while also contributing to an erosion of a positive sense of self. Further, when we overextend our energy (physical, psychological and spiritual energy) we increase our risks for physical illness. As such, it's important that we internalize just how the Maiden–Virgin Goddesses extend themselves—they reinvigorate their energy by ensuring they do enough for themselves *first*, then they have the momentum and the strength to do for others. We must strive for balanced caring whereby we give to others, but recognize that it is first critical to nourish ourselves. As such consider crafting a ritual to help heal the patriarchal instinct to self-sacrifice.

A Solar Maiden–Virgin Story of Mabon

(September 21–23, Western Hemisphere)

Our Maiden–Virgin Goddess has given a large burst of energy toward the world beneath her to bring the last grains into ripeness and to provide a pulse of energy to ensure abundance and resources carry through the winter months (in preparation for her own descent). She continues to mature and to learn how to keep her core self while engaging deeply and meaningfully with others. And so she comes to the Autumnal Equinox.

Her energy is waning and she has just enough to bring about the ripening of the fruits of the year. The light will markedly shorten after this day, the air will cool as the Sun rises lower and lower in the sky, and life will return to gestation. But not quite yet… As she matures into a new sense of Maidenself, she becomes her compassionate self—she focuses on ensuring the hearth and home are strong to carry those who dwell

☽○☾ Symbol & Ritual Tip

Mabon raises the question of what is home? When we first think of this question we tend to consider the "home is where the heart is", but we also have connotations of family, permanence, stability, and issues of ownership. Home often connotes achievement—something earned and gained through effort, whether in relationships (and thus the concept is transportable and only related to human and nonhuman companions) or through cultural expressions (such as monetary success). Within the Western world having a home has become synonymous with being successful. Further, many people worldwide lose their homes through financial loss, land seizure, or more dramatic means (natural disasters or cultural violence). This is a day to guard against this assumption whereby your value as a person is linked with how much you have earned or accomplished. If you find yourself faced with housing losses or find yourself identifying your self-esteem and worth with your house, consider crafting a ritual on this day to free yourself from cultural traps and to return to the core of the Maiden–Virgin Goddess who reminds us our body is our primary home and the Earth our primal and constant shelter.

beneath her through the dark time of her transformation. She will not abandon life, but gradually reminds those who dwell below that we must all stand on our own two feet and she will ensure we have the necessary skills to do this. She is Hestia and Vesta, the Maiden Goddess of the Hearth and Home.

Solar Maiden–Virgin Mystery Rites of Mabon

The Maiden–Virgin Goddess is starting to depart. Her presence is waning and so she encourages us to join with others to seek new sources of energy (self-sufficiency through cooperation, mutualism, and symbiosis). She does this by allocating her energy to our homes (our communities we are tied to), rather than our persons alone. She embraces the whole of our house and all who enter in, rather than directing energy into each individual. Thus she encourages us to see ourselves as expanded, just as she has come to see herself. She does not exist solely, but exists within the whole and the whole exists within her. She is returning to her connections to her Mother and her Grandmother. She is becoming aware of her life cycle.

We are at the feast of the First Fruits and the time of thanksgiving and reflecting on what we have achieved and how others have helped us. This is a time for expressing the unsaid thanks to our mothers, fathers, grandparents, friends and lovers who have helped us clarify who we are and have given us energy. This is a time of seeing ourselves as part of a larger whole. We come to the awareness that we can be unique and complete alone, as well as within a larger group. We most commonly host a feast for those who have supported us and who have contributed to our positive development. Our rituals focus toward gratefulness and prosperity. We are focused on transcending the self—rising outside of the psychological and spiritual boundaries of self to include the wider world. Our ritual life focuses on honoring this new humanistic identity; however it is also important to recognize at this time that your success has also been afforded by many nonhuman beings (through food, companionship, materials, and through the very production of oxygen in the Earth). As such, this is also a day where we can transcend our human focus—we can craft what is known as an ecological self. We can honor, not only our human ancestors, but all the many nonhuman (plant and animal) spirits who have come to our aid over the years.

A Solar Maiden–Virgin Story of Samhain

(October 21, Western Hemisphere)

The Maiden–Virgin Goddess cannot stop her development. This is a time of transformation and change. She has remained strong in who she is—

☽ ○ ☾

she is certain in her talents and skills. She has learned of her capacities to support life and now she craves something else. Her Sun is waning and the days are shortening. She feels the pressure of growth—something is ending and waiting for a new beginning. She accepts that she is becoming something new, something different—a different kind of sun. She is transforming into the Great Mother—her maiden self is dying.

She is Sól–Sunna, the Sun Goddess who dies to become the Mother Goddess. She is Persephone who must reenter the underworld to become the wife–mother of the dead. She is Epona, the Maiden Goddess who transforms Herself into a Horse to guide the souls to the afterlife. She is the Maiden–Virgin end and dies to herself to become reborn. In her death, she gives the last of her energy to light our paths during our most challenging of times. She becomes the Maiden–Virgin who is tested, who is courageous and unyielding—she faces the darkening days as Andraste and Anat. She is providence and war—she is unyielding and without fear. She faces her transformation fully.

Solar Maiden–Virgin Mystery Rites of Samhain

At Samhain, we come to the end of the Solar Maiden–Virgin cycle. Here the Maiden retreats into the destiny of her development. She must mature, just as all of us come to a critical and defining moment of transformation in our lives. We come to the crossroads—and as Persephone turns to Hecate to aid her in her journey in the underworld, we too turn to our elders. We honor our ancestors, our mothers and fathers, and those who have passed on during the year. We honor our moments of transformation, both the trials and the times of ease. We honor our strength and courage to shine in the year. We light candles in honor of these and in reflection of the transforming sun as she moves from Maiden–Virgin to Mother.

This is a mystical day where we allow ourselves to be transformed. We engage in rituals that tap into our subconscious, such as divination, channeling, journeywork. We recognize that as the Maiden–Virgin Goddess moves into the underworld, the door between the seen and unseen world is thin. We protect our homes from unwanted energy and spirits and to secure our stead for the darkening days ahead.

A wonderful ritual for this day is a ceremonial crossing over our own threshold in celebration of our growth and development. This may be done in a doorway or in the movement between two sacred circles set up to touch each other. In one circle is our Maiden–Virgin self—our Unconquerable Self who has grown in the year. In this circle we contemplate all we have done and what we had to let go. We then cross into the other circle where we contemplate how we have been transformed and where we will go from here. We contemplate the underworld and dig deep into core truths of ourselves that we have discovered and that may or may not be difficult for us to hear. We gather the energy and speed of the mystical horse to encourage us to move forward and deeper. And we experience our core strength, the Warrior Maidens who surround us as we return to the center. When celebrating with others, the group keeps the circle of the present, allowing each member to cross over into the other. Whereby the first member represents Sunna (She should be the High Priestess of the group or the group's elder), the dying Sun who will in turn guide the way; while the participants who follow are those who reflect Persephone; finally the last participant to cross reflects Anat, the Maiden Goddess of caution, providence, and war. She should be the Priestess or the second most elder of the group. Once all are in the second circle, the group can engage in divination to see what direction their unique transformations will occur and read stories or poems of women standing at the crossroads.

❀

There are a host of variations that you can explore through the year when developing rituals and celebrations for each of the solar Maiden–Virgin sacred days. Goddess traditions thrive on creativity and spontaneity and so it is important to allow your own intuition to guide you. The information in this chapter reflects only one possible story thread. To get you started in your own crafting of your sacred calendar here are some general tips.

- ☽ If you work alone, keep it personal and reflective of where you are in the moment. Look for ways to augment or strengthen positives in your life rather than focus on what is lacking. Often times what is lacking simply reflects the need to attend to what we have and to strengthen our innate skills. While banishing energy and looking for prosperity are important, focus your ritual life on building on what you have and who you are. This will also help you increase your awareness of who you are.

- ☽ If you work in a group, take time as a group to discuss where everyone is at *prior* to each celebration. Look for common themes and shared experiences to craft the ritual. Additionally, you'll want to give vocal space for each member to express their own unique struggles—this can be done through creative projects such as poetry, song, or artistic work. Group honoring of each person's uniqueness can go a long way to affirming each person's Solar Maiden–Virgin self.

- ☽ Incorporate ritual items from outdoors found on walks—this brings an immediacy to the rituals that links them to the wider source of energy in Nature. Humanmade objects are fine, but the Goddess dwells in life—finding objects that She has made directly carries a more potent energy.

- ☽ While rituals often seek to craft the experience of an otherworldly event, to designate an area that sits between two worlds; I encourage you to explore in vivo experiences in wild spaced. Sometimes simply being in "nature" is foreign enough for us that our consciousness is transformed. Further, this reminds us how vivid and present the Goddess is in the world around us. It also fosters a more ecologically balanced perspective.

- Remythologize. Don't be afraid to rework myths and stories of Goddesses if they are defined by patriarchy. Much of the artifacts of womanness have to be reconstructed. Women have been silenced for a long period of time. Also don't be afraid to utilize contemporary songs or literature that may not mention a Goddess, but speaks of the themes of a specific Goddess.

- Keep it simple. We tend to get very complicated in our rituals and they look great on paper, but often times when it comes to actually performing the ritual we tend to forget things or rely so heavily on a script that we no longer experience the power of a ritual. Most rituals within antiquity and prehistory were simple and designed to create visceral changes in consciousness (drumming, whirling dances, repetitive chanting, incense, etc.). Focus on meaningful repetition and awakening the specific senses, rather than on recitation of lengthy passages or movement through diverse ritual behavior. If you do recite keep it simple and rhythmic; if you're in a group you can expand this into a vivid story that awakens the imagination.

☽ ○ ☾

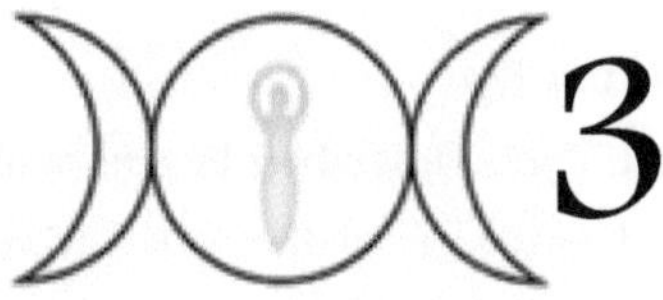

3

Now close your eyes and try to see the moon in your head.
—Zsuzsanna Budapest

The Lunar Maiden

> But tonight the earth's attention has been recaptured by this angel-hair sliver of white, stark against the blue serge sky.... The women gathered here tonight herald this, the moon's reappearance, and partake of its rebirth in a ritual of new beginning.[1]

The changing face of the Moon encourages us to examine our own changes throughout the month. The solar–harvest celebrations generally mark substantial developmental cycles and changes: events that are noticeable and often dramatic. In contrast, the Moon reflects our emotional tides, our psychic changes, the intimacy of our relationships, our hormonal cycles, and tracks our day-to-day development. Lunar rites are a time when we can connect to the Goddess energy to create effective change in our lives and personal development. They tend to be deeply personal and often mystical in nature, making them ideal for individuals to solitarily engage in. Within a group setting, these days can be perfect for more shamanistic rituals that allow for journeywork and rites that encourage mystical communion.

Celebrating a sacred lunar year provides ample opportunity for four diverse wheels: the Lunar–Maiden, the Lunar–Mother, and the Lunar–Crone, and the Lunar–Dark Goddess. In this chapter, we'll specifically focus on the Lunar–Maiden wheel, also known as the Bright Maiden.[2] For

☽○☾ Symbol & Ritual Tip

You'll find that each cycle described begins with the January moon in keeping with our discussion on the Solar Maiden–Virgin. This is an ideal starting place for those of you who facilitate coven/grove work. However, if you are working alone, I strongly encourage you to develop your own beginning and ending cycle for the Lunar year that best suits your own needs as these cycles are so deeply personal. For example, you may wish to start the new year with the Moon of your birthday month. When you intuit or personalize your own schedule this also increases the power of the day and your own mystical experience.

each of the wheels, Goddess-based High Priestess Z. Budapest encourages individuals seeking to connect with the Moon to create their own permanent Lunar altar. This is a deeply personal altar that changes with the moon's cycles, writing:

> Create a nature table with a white cloth, silvery things, sea creatures such as shells, pictures of the Moon, and images of the Goddess of the Moon. Keep some water in a pretty dish on the altar, put salt in another. Obtain silver candles and use them as your meditation candles....refresh it daily... by putting fresh flowers or decorations on it.[3]

With the altar in place, individuals can easily begin working with the power of the Moon and the Goddess energy instilled within this power. I additionally recommend that individuals always have a journal on this altar as the Lunar time is often full of revelation and personal insight.

When we specifically turn our attention to the Lunar–Maiden calendar it is a calendar of new beginnings and rebirths. It is a time of enthusiasm and launching into new projects. It is a period of optimism and excitement. Like all Lunar rites, the Lunar–Maiden calendar is a time when we can engage in ritual actions that facilitate our personal growth. And it is celebrated at the first crescent moon of each month. In this fashion, there are 12 opportunities to awaken the Bright Maiden Goddess energy within yourself and in your life. Each month is an opportunity to awaken a different aspect and energy pattern of the Maiden–Virgin Goddess in your life. There are three ways in which you can work to determine the sacred Maiden meaning of each month: (a) Farmer's Almanac[4] (comprised of traditional Native American moons); (b) Celtic Tree names; and (c) self-named. We will begin to look at in depth in this chapter.

Native American Moons of the Almanac

Published in the United States continuously since 1818, the Farmer's Almanac has long been the companion for all-things related to seasonal cycles. In particular, over the years, they have continued to preserve the names given to the Lunar cycles by indigenous Americans. These Lunar names are associated with regional observations with made over generations of relying on the natural cycles of the environment for sustenance. Over time, these traditional names have been adapted by a large number of Neopagan practitioners in their Lunar Rites. If you live outside North America, discover how indigenous cultures in your region defined lunar cycles.

☽ Wolf or Old Moon (January): This marks the first winter moon in the Western hemisphere and it is a moon associated with the unpredictable wilds—where the hand of fate seems more present and the drive to pull in one's resources more pronounced. Within a Goddess-based Framework we might consider this moon as either a *Sister Wolf Moon* or *Grandmother Moon.* Wolves form strong bonds of sisterhood and when the alpha female gives birth, all the Maiden–Virgin female wolves will sympathetically produce milk. This insures that the pups will be fostered throughout the seasons. It is a time of sympathy (often mislabeled as empathy) and strengthening one's resources through support systems. It is a time when we look toward our sisters who have come to help us and express our gratitude. We also look toward the "sister" and "handmaiden" Goddesses who have sheltered, supported, empowered, and rescued. These are the Goddesses of great strength and often little egoism. Their myths abound with messages of cooperation and they are often endowed with potent magic and great skills. They are the Sisters whose strengths are most needed during times of paucity and harshness. For us, it is a time of acclimating to the changing landscape and the cold. If we consider the Maiden-Lunar aspects of the first crescent, it is a moon of the wild self—something increasingly mysterious to our encultured lives. It is a moon that celebrates our "creatureness". It is Artemis or Bendis's moon. Sisters who stalk the untamed wilderness with boars and wolves. Sisters who watched over the Mothers and provide women with valuable ways of being complete and solitary. She is our unruly self, our power selves, our thirst for discovery of what lies beneath the newly fallen snows. It is the time of the Sister Goddesses, the Zorya, star goddesses who hold back the destruction from the universe and called upon for defense and protection from harmful energies that may abound in life. She reminds us that we are complex and full beings, while also reminding us that we are intimately linked to all life through sisterhood. When we come to our discussion of the Crone, we'll look at how this lunar time is a Grandmother Moon.

☽ Snow or Hunger Moon (February). This is a moon of the deep winter. It is a time when the snows are thick and heavy. In northern, North American cultures it was a time when food was scarce and there was a reliance on stored grains and hunting. It was a time of hunkering down and going with less. This is a survivor moon, whereby we come to acknowledge our capacity to withstand our own hungers; what we must go without to weather the storms. If we consider the Lunar–Maiden aspects of this moon, we are being asked to understand what we still do not know or have not learned. We are being asked to recognize that there are elements of our life where we must entrust to others to help us. While it is the moon of our limitations, it is also a moon that encourages us to recognize that we can weather any storm. We are protected. It is the moon of Laumé, the Latvian Maiden Fairy Goddess known as the "White Lady" who protects the poor and hungry.

☽ Worm, Crow, Crust, or Sap Moon (March): When the moon turns to this time of year, it is the time when saps begin to flow in the trees, breaking from their winter freeze. It is a time when the icy crust that girds the land begins to melt and crack. It is a time when worms begin to emerge from their wintering dens beneath the deep earth as the new rains fall. It is a time when the trickster crow can be heard throughout the woods; a carrion bird who reflects the clearing out of the "dead" winter and bringing it into new spring life—it is also a time of psychic strength. In Lunar–Maiden meaning of this moon, it is a time of cleaning house and making difficult choices. In this aspect of the Lunar time, it is a time of The Morrígan, the Irish Goddess of War and Death. She is the Goddess of Strength, resolve, and courage. In the softer, flowing aspect of the Moon—in its springtime anticipation, it is a time of unleashing your creativity, passion, and fertility: getting those juices flowing. In this aspect it is the time of the goddess Uzume, the Japanese goddess of passion, fertility, and lust. The one who dances before the cave of Amaterasu to lure her out. It is a time of the Maiden-Creatrix Ataecina, an Iberian goddess of spring rebirth, fertility, and nature.

☽ Pink, Sprouting, Fish, or Egg Moon (April): This is a spring moon, when the first hints of the growing season appear. The world literally pinkens with the first blossoms of many flowering trees, such as the cherry. It is a time when flowers begin to sprout. With the full thaw of the rivers and lakes, the fish have become accessible. It is a time when birds lay their eggs. In the Lunar–Maiden aspects of this moon, it is a time when we can begin to feel the first flush of optimism and excitement. We feel energized and ready to direct ourselves toward new projects. It is a time of Tomam, the Siberian Goddess of the Birds—she is the Goddess that welcomes the return of the wildlife to the land and the birds to the increasingly warmer weather. It is also the time of Pandora, the Maiden Creatrix Goddess known as "giver of all, all endowed" and the giver of blessings. She is the Goddess who brings the earth into its fullness, with the balancing cycles of life and death. She is the keeper of hope, guarding it closely to her. Hope is the most closely guarded of all emotions and the most important we have to travel our journey with.

☽ Flower, Corn Planting, or Milk Moon (May): This is a moon for planting the grains that will sustain oneself through the fall and winter months. It is the time when mammals begin to nurse their young and flowers have started to widely bloom. It is a full -flushed landscape of realized goals. Within the Lunar–Maiden aspects of this moon it is a time of fruition and of nurturing that which is newly born. It is the delicate time where new goals are just beginning to manifest. We are most vulnerable to outside criticism at this time. It is a time when we benefit from the Maiden Goddess Sirona, a goddess of the healing springs who encourages growth and nurtures the development of children and child-states. With Sirona, we are buffered from negativity that would undermine our newly fledged growth. It is the time of Hygeia and Jurās Māte, the Goddesses of healing, snakes, spells and charm work to ensure our healthy success.

☽ ○ ☾

- ☽ Strawberry or Rose Moon (June): This is the moon when the strawberries come to fruit and roses bloom. It is a heady and fragrant time of year. Summer is coming and heat is rising. It is the second blossoming moon and the landscape is a myriad of colors. Similar to our previous moon, this is a moon of our goals. Our fledging goals of the previous moon have matured and are fruiting. We are stronger in our courage to pursue our goals and we can share our optimism. Now is the time for us to take care to not lose sight of our goals; rather it is a time of nurturing them. In this we may turn to Kuan-Yin, the goddess of compassion. In her we learn not only how to direct our own nurturing energy toward our goals, but keep it balanced by nurturing others in their own pursuits and optimism. This is also a whimsical time when Faery energy flourishes and we may tap into this through Zana, the Balkan maiden Forest Fairy Goddess.

- ☽ Buck, Thunder, or Hay Moon (July): This moon is the time when hay is ready for harvesting—casting a golden-green color along fields. It is a time when summer storms billow up late in the day as the heat builds, leading to the crashing of thunder. It is a time when bucks' antlers are solidifying to show their prowess during the coming mating season. In the Lunar-Maiden meanings, this is a time of emotional upheaval and sudden bursts of emotional energy. It can be a time of the Eryines the maiden sister goddesses of anger and vengeance. In this capacity, it is a time of learning to work with one's own anger. It may also be a time of "selling" what one has brought to fruition—getting oneself out there. In this fashion, it is a time of showing off one's antlers, one's symbols of potency. As such it may be a period of Peitho, the Maiden goddess of persuasion.

☽ ○ ☾

- ☽ Sturgeon, Green Corn, or Grain Moon (August): This is a time when corn is ripened and grains are ready for harvesting. Sturgeons are widely available for fishing and the harvest has arrived, a time of preparing for the winter ahead. It is a time of good fortune and the fruits of all one's labors are now coming into being. We are tied to fate this month—trusting in the natural world's processes that our sustenance will come to fruition. We enter a time where we reap what we have sown. In Lunar–Maiden times this is the Moon of the Norns, the Norse sisters of Fate; it is the Moon of Tyche and Fortuna, where we look to increase our luck (not only through our work with them, but through our own hard work and careful planning). It is the time of Nortia, the Etruscan goddess of Fate, and Ananké and Karta, all the fate goddesses. This is the month where we put our trust in the forces outside of us with equal fervor as we revivify our trust in ourselves.

- ☽ Harvest Moon (September): The moon is bright and dominant in this month; it was a moon associated with working longer into the night to gather the last grains before they rot on the field. In the Lunar–Maiden aspects, it is a time of Luna. Luna is the sister of Aurora, the Solar Maiden goddess of the Dawn. This is a time of gathering what we need. It is a time when we have a chance to look at what the fates have taught us in the month before and gather all our resources to meet the upcoming challenges. Luna shines down on us to give us more time and energy to assess our supplies and gather. While Selene, the Titan Goddess of the moon races through the sky with her boars or white horses to seek out her lover. Reminding us that this moon is also a moon of intimacy and the dream of love. It is the time of Mayari, the Tagalog Moon Goddess, who lost her eye in a fight with her brother to ensure justice and equality for the inhabitants of the Earth. During the time of the moon, her power rises and we may look toward rituals that promote social justice and ensuring the sustenance for all.

☽ Hunter's Moon (October): This is the final moon of the year where it provides enough light for the last efforts to gather supplies for the winter. In particular, this is the month of gathering the supplies that protect the body and home—tribes hunted for leather and furs and meats were dried for later protein during the lean times to come. This is another month where the moon becomes the sole focus. In the Lunar–Maiden meaning, it is the time of Ilargi, the Basque Moon Goddess, daughter of the Earth Mother. Reminding us that our sustenance for the winter months is dependent upon the Earth and through the intercession of her Lunar–Maiden daughter, we are provided for. In this fashion, this moon reminds us of our interconnection and dependency upon the larger world around us, specifically the non -encultured world. We may also look to Pasiphae, a lunar deity and goddess of the bulls—whereby the "hunt" is a more intimate union—merging nonhuman with human; once more reminding us of our interdependency with the nonhuman world.

☽ Beaver or Frosty Moon (November): We come to the first moon of Autumn. Beavers are seen busily building their homes and damming rivers in preparation for the coming winter. The first frosts arrive and the temperatures drop. This is a moon where we begin to turn inward. The Lunar–Maiden aspects of this moon encourage us to redirect our attention inwardly. This is a magical month of increased psychic abilities and intuition. It is a month of preparation for the dreaming time. It is the month of descent. It is the month of Freya and Persephone. It is the time of Leucothea or Losna, the White Moon Goddess of the sea and prophecy. This Lunar–Maiden period is a time of developing our internal power of divination, prophecy, and the shamanic

☽ ○ ☾

journey to the lower world.

- ☽ Cold or Long Nights Moon (December): The month where dreaming continues. The days are short and cold. The trees are bare and the time spent in sleep is long. This is the time of the underworld—the journey to the lower realms. The land of ancestors, of psyche, of dreams, of gestation. In the Lunar–Maiden year, this is the time of Hel/Hella, the Norse goddess of the underworld, and of Kebechet, the ancient Egyptian goddess of the waters and underworld. We are moving away from our everyday pursuits and goals and into our core centers, where spirit resides. It is a time of reflection and putting to rest what has been unhealthy for us and divining new paths for us to embark upon with refreshed energy.

Celtic Tree Moons

Structuring your year along the Celtic Tree calendar is another mode of incorporating a goddess-mindful year (we'll be looking at the Coligny Calendar shortly). While the veracity of the Celtic Tree calendar is largely disputed in academic circles as being an imaginative construct of poet-scholar Robert Graves in his classic text *The White Goddess*, it has become a profound way of creating rites that are psychologically and ecologically cohesive and spiritually transformative. To begin orienting ourselves to the Celtic Tree calendar we need to understand three elements of it: the underlying poem it is based on (the *Cad Goddeu* or the "Battle of the Trees" which is a substantially different poem than what Graves reduces it to), the defined trees and their meanings, and the associations of these trees with "Song of Amergin" (translated by Robert Graves). We'll look at each of these sections and what we can spiritually glean from them and how they can serve to create a cohesive foundation to the unfolding year as it relates to a Lunar Maiden (we'll return to this

☽ ○ ☾

topic when we arrive to our discussion on the Lunar Mother and Lunar Crone).

The Battle of the Trees

Following is the complete text of the Battle of the Trees, Book of Taliessin VIII from *The Four Ancient Books of Whales* translated by William F. Skene (1868) with some modern adjustments made by me.

I have been in a multitude of shapes,
Before I assumed a consistent form.
I have been a sword, narrow, variegated,
I will believe when it is apparent.
I have been a tear in the air,
I have been the dullest of stars.
I have been a word among letters,
I have been a book in the origin.
I have been the light of lanterns
a year and a half.
I have been a continuing bridge,
over three scores abers[4]
I have been a course, I have been an eagle.
I have been a coracle[5] in the seas:
I have been compliant in the banquet.
I have been a drop in a shower;
I have been a sword in the grasp of the hand:
I have been a shield in battle.
I have been a string in a harp,
disguised for nine years.
In water, in foam.
I have been sponge in the fire,
I have been wood in the covert.
I am not he who will not sing of

a combat though small,
the conflict in the battle of Godeau of sprigs.
Against the Guledig of Prydain,[6]
there passed central horses,
fleets full of riches.
There passed an animal with wide jaws,
on in there were a hundred heads.
And a battle was contested
under the root of his tongue;
And another battle there is
in his eye.
A black sprawling toad,
with a hundred claws on it.
A snake speckled, crested.
A hundred souls through sin
shall be tormented in its flesh.
I have been in Caer Vevenir,
there hastened grass and trees,
minstrels were singing,
warrior-bands were wondering,[7]
at the exultation of the British,
that Gwydyon[8] effected.
There was a calling on the Creator,
upon Christ[9] for causes,
until when the Eternal
should deliver those whom he had made.
The Lord answered them,
through language and elements:
take the forms of the principal trees,
arranging yourselves in battle array,
and restraining the public.
Inexperienced in battle hand to band.
When the trees were enchanted,

☽ ○ ☾

in the expectation of not being trees,
the trees uttered their voices
from strings of harmony,
the disputes ceased.
Let us cut short heavy days,
a female restrained the din.
She came forth altogether lovely.
The head of the line, the head was a female.
The advantage of a sleepless cow[10]
would not make us give way.
The blood of men up to our thighs,
the greatest of demanding mental exertions
sported in the world.
And one has ended
from considering the deluge,
and Christ crucified,
and the day of judgment near at hand.
The alder-trees, the head of the line
formed the advanced position.
The willows and quicken-trees
came late to the army.
Plum-trees, that are scarce,
unlonged for of men.
The elaborate medlar trees,
the objects of contention.
The prickly rose-bushes,
against a host of giants;
The raspberry brake did
what is better failed
for the security of life.
Privet and woodbine
and ivy on its front,
Like furze to the combat

☽ ○ ☾

91 the cherry-tree was provoked.
92 The birch, notwithstanding his high mind,
93 was late before he was arrayed.
94 Not because of his cowardice,
95 but on account of his greatness.
96 The laburnum held in mind,
97 that your wild nature was foreign.
98 Pine-trees in the porch,
99 the chair of disputation,
100 by me greatly exalted,
101 in the presence of kings.
102 The elm with his retinue,
103 did not go aside a foot;
104 he would fight with the center,
105 and the flanks, and the rear.
106 Hazel-trees, it was judged
107 that ample was thy mental exertion.
108 The privet, happy his lot,
109 the bull of battle, the lord of the world.
110 Morawag and Morydd
111 were made prosperous in pines.
112 Holly, it was tinted with green,
113 He was the hero.
114 The hawthorn, surrounded by prickles,
115 with pain at his hand.
116 The aspen-wood has been topped,
117 it was topped in battle.
118 The fern that was plundered.
119 The broom, in the advance of the army,
120 in the trenches he was hurt.
121 The gorse did not do well,
122 notwithstanding let it overspread.
123 The heath was victorious, keeping off on all sides.

The common people were charmed,
during the proceeding of the men.
The oak quickly moving,
before him, tremble heaven and earth.
A valiant door-keeper against an enemy,
his name is considered.
The blue-bells combined
and caused a consternation.
In rejecting, were rejected,
others, that were perforated.
Pear-trees, the best intruders
in conflict of the plain.
A very wrathful wood,
the chestnut is bashful,
the opponent of happiness,
the jet has become black,
the mountain has become crooked,
the woods have become a kiln,
existing formerly in the great seas,
since was heard the shout:—
The tops of the birch covered us with leaves,
and transformed us, and changed our faded state.
The branches of the oak have ensnared us
From the Gwarchan of Maelderw[11].
Laughing on the side of the rock,
the lord is not of ardent nature.
not of mother and father,
when I was made,
did my Creator create me.
Of nine-formed faculties,
of the fruit of fruits,
of the fruit of the primordial God,
of primroses and blossoms of the hill,

of the flowers of trees and shrubs.
of earth, of an earthly course,
when I was formed.
Of the flower of nettles,
Of the water of the ninth wave[12].
I was enchanted by Math,
Before I became immortal;
I was enchanted by Gwydon,[13]
the great purifier of the Britons,
of Eurwys of Euron,
of Euron, of Modron[14].
Of five battalions of scientific ones,
Teachers, children of Math.
When the removal occurred,
I was enchanted by the Guledig.[15]
When he was half-burnt,
I was enchanted by the sage
of sages, in the primordial world.
When I had a being;
when the host of the world was in dignity,
the bard was accustomed to benefits.
To the song of praise I am inclined, which the tongue recites,
I played in the twilight,
I slept in the purple;
I was truly in the enchantment
With Dylan, the son of the wave.[16]
In the circumference , in the middle,
between the knees of kings,
scattering spears not keen,
from heaven when came,
to the great deep, floods,
in the battle there will be
four score hundreds,

that will divide according to their will.
They are neither older nor younger,
than myself in their divisions.
A wonder, Canhwr are born, every one of nine hundred.[17]
He was with me also,
with my sword spotted with blood.
Honor was allotted me
by the Lord, and protection where he was.
If I come to where the boar was killed,
he will compose, he will decompose,
he will form languages.
The strong-handed gleamer, his name,
With a gleam he rules his numbers,
They would spread out in a flame,
when I shall go on high.
I have been a speckled snake on the hill,
I have been a viper in the Llyn.
I have been a bill-hook crooked that cuts,
I have been a ferocious spear
With my chasuble[18] and bowl
I will prophesy not badly,
four score smokes
On every one what will bring.
Five battalions of arms
will be caught by my knife;
six steeds of yellow hue
a hundred times better is
my cream-colored steed,
swift as the seagull
which will not pass
between the sea and the shore.
Am I not pre-eminent in the field of blood?
Over it are a hundred chieftains.

☽ ○ ☾

Crimson, the gem of my belt,
gold my shield border.
There has not been born, in the gap,
that has been visiting me,
except Goronwy[19],
from the dales of Edrywy.
Long white my fingers,
it is long since I have been a herdsman.
I travelled in the earth,
before I was a proficient in learning.
I travelled, I made a circuit,
I slept in a hundred islands.
A hundred Caers I have dwelt in.
Druids,
Declare to Arthur,
what is there more early
than I that they sing of.
And once is come
from considering the deluge.
and Christ crucified,
and the day of future doom.[20]
A golden gem in a golden jewel.
I am splendid
and shall be wanton
from the oppression of the metal-workers.[21]

Taking a cursory look at this text on the surface it feels as if there is little to do with moons, cycles, Goddesses and spirituality at all, and far more to do with mythic-heroic narration of battle interspersed with choppy Christian editorializing. And I think the poem could very easily be read surfacely in this direction; however, after spending time with the text I think we can gather some important information that can be inclusive to a Celtic Tree calendar—outside from the positioning of trees (including non-Ogham ones) to suggest the unfolding battle of the year. Let's explore.

One of the first elements of the poem that stands out is the voice of the poet. Written in the first person ("I") throughout we have a markedly overt competing narrative to the overlaying Christian God/Creator. In this text, the "I" is the creator and the "I" is a slippery immanent and eminent being. The "I" dwells within all things. This speaks to the concept of Awen, which refers to poetic inspiration and creation. The author, the manifest of Awen emerges before the Christian God and dwells within that which is created by the hands of humans, as well as within the bodies of other living beings. It has garnered the experience of being all things. This could be seen as exemplifying the transformative process of being creative, being a storyteller, crafting a narrative. In this definitional space, it reminds us that all rituals throughout a year tell a story and move us into new spaces of being. We are the storytellers and become all that is created in these narratives in intimate and energetic ways. This potent "I" begins and ends the narrative epic. This provides us with a further elucidation of the meaning of a Celtic Tree Calendar—it begins and ends with I, an internal spirit that develops its creative potency—overcoming all conflicts of self, society, spirit, and relationships, transforming them into a new re-birthed I. In this fashion, we can readily define a Celtic Tree Calendar of the year as one that traces this cycle for ourselves. Within a Maiden Lunar Cycle, this would reflect the development of and transformation of the Maiden, the Virginal Self, moving toward the genesis of dedication or commitment. The Maiden voyage embarks on newness, new projects, new edges of self identity, new skills, new relationships and develops these with deepening intimacy, enchantment, wonder, and potency until the final act of transformation into Mother—whereby what is new is birthed into the world as something separate from self.

As the poem moves from the central narrator who claims their authority, we move into the battle of the trees. We encounter two important points in the outset. The first is the trees produce harmony upon their initial emergence. They immediately quell the initial din. Thus suggesting an important element of our understanding of the natural world as one that fosters balance. From this balanced state of stillness, a great She, a Lady emerges, who stands at the head of the battle unmoved. In British Isle lore, as with much of wider European lore, the most potent mediators of battle and war, are Goddesses. Merging their mythic capacity to transform fate, oversee death and resurrection, and gain the truth, when we examine this text, we begin to see the strands of the great Goddess of memory and creation emerge. Here we find the Great Goddess, Brigantia. We know little about her under this name, but substantially more under the name of Brigid, the goddess of knowledge, healing, peace, and inspiration. Brigantia, patron and spiritual foundress of the Brythons (Britains) likely reflects a more substantial blending of warrior -healer, much like we might see Artemis or Freyja. Both of whom manifested Virginal-Maiden powers. Another way of viewing the emergence of the Divine Female in this verse (62-67) is to also consider the heroic, warrior queens of Great Britain, such as Boadicea—who led a great army into battle against Roman occupation. In this we are reminded of the power of womyness to stand in the face of terror and war and fight for justice. In this, we can consider the Celtic Year as one that also reminds us to apply our Lunar Maiden selves toward a righteous year, meaning a year of clarity, justice, and courage.

Beginning in line 148 we encounter the potential identities of the narrator and these are of tantamount importance for women of the Goddess and of the Maiden Lunar Cycle, as well as support for the notion of an underlying cyclical role of a year of rites. Beginning in this verse, we encounter the divine I that pre-dates the Christian god, so much so that the author adamantly notes that they exist prior to this god—a subversive element retained within a Christianized text. There are two divine figures that emerge within this section: the great Lunar Queen Goddess Arianrhod and the Solar Spring Mother Goddess Blodeuwedd. Within a Lunar Maiden discussion, we'll focus on Arianrhod.

☽ ○ ☾

Arianrhod comes to us from the Mabinogian as the virginal, independent queen born of the primordial creatrix, Dôn. She is a goddess of war, warcraft, justice, fate, and magic. She may bring about blessings or cursors. We learn in the myth of the parthogenic birth of her divine sons, Lleu and Dylan, that she rejects all relational ties. This primordial aloneness that she guards likely reflects the desire to remain clear-minded and empowered. With her son of the waves, we could also link her to the sea—a powerful oceanic presence, subservient to no one. When Math's rod penetrates her with his magical rod, she gives birth to two sons, Lleu (the Bright One) and Dylan (the Son of the Wave). Lleu is challenged by Arinrhod in three ways: the denial of a name, the denial of physical prowess, and the denial of a wife—setting the stage for his heroic journey. In contrast, Dylan, whose name closely resembles the etymology of his grandmother, is baptized in the primordial sea where he magically shapeshifts to become a fish.[22]

If we consider that Arianrhod is the narrator who becomes all things created living and dead, enchants the trees, who stands at the gates of the battle, and who charges the Druids to correctly witness the poem, it stands to reasons that we cold also consider the deeper meaning of her three curses or *tynged*, her marks of fate upon each of us as we deepen our understanding of our deeper Lunar Maiden years. In this I recommend for those working a Lunar Maiden year to consider meeting the challenges of what I call "Arianrhod's Tynged"—these may also be broken down into a three-year cycle or modified to fit a three-year Maiden, Mother, Crone cycle.

☽ Name Tynged: Arianrhod establishes the names of all beings. This reflects more than simply a name, as it reflects the deeper elements of ourselves. It reflects our introspection and a recognition of who we are meant to be; who we are gifted to be in our core. Rites during the year would be focused on illuminating our sacred self; this may even include rituals of receiving a sacred name.

☽ ○ ☾

- ☽ Battle Tynged: while the myths are patriarchal, it is clear that Arianrhod was linked to warcraft, but we can think of this in more spiritual terms. Each of us face struggles in our lives that requires us to battle through, that requires us to be armed with strengths to cope with these events. When we incorporate this into our spiritual year, we are looking to identify our challenges and seek out our strengths to help us better cope with these challenges. We can approach this as challenges within the year or more lifelong "battles". As in the Battle of the Trees, no battle is too small to be told and discussed.

- ☽ Relational Tynged: Arianrhod can compose or decompose our relationships, allowing them to flourish or become constrained. During the year we can work on our relationship skills—bringing our spiritual mindfulness into our everyday relationships. No relationship is too small to become a manifestation of the spirit. Each relationship in the course of our sacred year is an opportunity to merge with the Goddess.

☽○☾ Symbol & Ritual Tip

When we examine the Lunar Year from as a Silver Wheel, we are given an opportunity to honor Arianrhod by working on our three challenges. If you do not wish to work along the Ogham Lunar cycles, you can work on these three challenges in a three-part cycle of the year: Fall as a time of name-seeking; Winter as a time of battle-testing; and Summer as a time of sacred relating. The three-part year cycle is consistent with British Isle traditions for those of you working with Celtic energies.

The final element of the poem that is worth examining from a spiritual and ritual perspective is the shamanistic element of consciousness transformation and merging within other beings and the linkage be-

☽ ○ ☾

tween self and plant spirits. While this text is not about shamanstic journeying, for those reading examining the trees within the poem from a perspective of merging one's consciousness with these species as totemic guides. Additionally, as many of the plants in the poem correspond to Bach Flowers, individuals may also consider the Bach Flower properties or include this in ritual healing activities throughout the year.

The Celtic Trees: Ogham

Celtic Tree Moon cycles are somewhat more complicated than the traditional American moon cycles in that the extra days that are accumulated within a 29-day lunar calendar are incorporated within the cycle to correspond to 13 months. As there are ample texts to explore the Oghams and in turn the tree meanings, I will only provide a brief overview. In my reference section of this text, you'll find some further recommended resources. I also encourage you to explore the Battle of the Trees to augment your understanding as the poetic vision of the trees illustrates how the ancient Celts perceived the strengths or powers of these trees. These may further inform your ritual structure or any issues you might wish to work on during the associated month..

Birch (12/24–next New Moon): signifies the moon of inception—this may be seen as Maiden–Virgin Goddesses who are fresh in their youth and vitality (Artemis, Diana for example).

Rowan (January): signifies the moon of vision—Maiden goddesses that reflect psychic skills and creativity may be called upon here (Freyja, the Norse Goddess–shamaness). In our poem we find the narrator claims the skill of prophecy.

Ash (February): signifies the moon of floods, the deluge—this is similar to the Quickening moon associated with Dianic traditions and reflects the impending flood of birth fluids, as well as the flowing milk of sheep at Imbolc. As a maiden aspect, it can be seen as the Maiden unleashing her creative juices into the earth—this may be seen as a time of Pandora, the Goddess to unleashes life and death, blessings and healings into the earth, as such this is a powerful time when one must be conscious of their potency.

Alder (March): signifies the moon of utility, think practical and pragmatic! This is a moon of the Maiden goddesses that help us get things done, such as Peitho, the Goddess of Persuasion. In our poem, we find both trees and divine goddess alike still the battle, quieting the din of conflict.

Willow (April): signifies the moon of enchantment, a time of whimsy and joyfulness. In our poem we find the emergence of enchant play a significant role in describing the narrator and their capacity to do magic. We might consider the Faery queen of the woods, Zana.

Hawthorn (May): signifies the moon of restraint, we might consider restraint the issue of compassion—through compassion we can act with restraint and calm. As such we might consider this the time of Kuan-Yin.

Oak (June): signifies the moon of strength, this is the time of Bendis (an aspect of Her) and the Morrigan, the goddesses of war and courage.

Holly (July): signifies the moon of unity and protection—this is the time of harmony and protection, where we might encounter Laumé.

Hazel (August): signifies the moon of wisdom—we might turn toward Hygeia during this moon, whereby to become a healer, we must be wise.

Vine (September): signifies the moon of exhilaration, we might find Uzume here and other Maiden's of fertility, passion, and lust.

Ivy (October): signifies the moon of harmony & balance—we may turn to the Fate goddesses in this time, seeking to understand the wheel of life, whereby what goes up, comes down, what is given is received.

Reed (11/1–11/26): signifies the moon of security and during this time we may turn to Sirona.

Elder (11/27–12/23): signifies the moon of completion, finally we may turn to Luna and Selene, the maiden Goddesses who reflect the fulfillment of the moon—the entire moon cycle is embodied by them and all its facets.

The Song of Amergin

The text of the Song of Amergin has often been associated with each of the Oghams, including those of the Celtic Tree Calendar. Several lines of the song have been specifically linked to the Trees of the Celtic Calendar. I've identified these lines in bold. When we consider this song in association with the year, we can look at it from the symbolic lessons we must acquire as we move through the year. Lets examine the song.

1 [Birch]	**I am a stag: of seven tines,**
2 [Rowan]	**I am a flood: across a plain,**
3 [Ash]	**I am a wind: on a deep lake,**
4 [Alder]	**I am a tear: the Sun lets fall,**

☽ ○ ☾

5 [Willow]	**I am a hawk: above the cliff,**
6	I am a thorn: beneath the nail,
7 [Hawthorn]	**I am a wonder: among flowers,**
8 [Oak]	**I am a sorcerer: who but I**
9	**Sets the cool head aflame with smoke?**
10 [Holly]	**I am a spear: that roars for blood,**
11 [Hazel]	**I am a salmon: in a pool,**
12	I am a lure: from paradise,
13 [Vine]	**I am a hill: where poets walk,**
14 [Ivy]	**I am a boar: ruthless and red,**
15 [Reed]	**I am a breaker: threatening doom,**
16 [Elder]	**I am a tide: that drags to death,**
17	I am an infant: who but I
18	peeps from the unhewn dolmen, arch?
19	I am the womb: of every holt,
20	I am the blaze: on every hill,
21	I am the queen: of every hive,
22	I am the shield: for every head,
23	I am the tomb: of every hope.

☽○☾ Symbol & Ritual Tip

Another way to consider this song is to recognize it is a song of affirmation—it is a statement of what constitutes the ideal Self. As such, I encourage you to expand your lens beyond the lunar affiliations to the entire context of the song and consider how you affirm (make real) each of the elements in your own life. You may wish to consider stating one of the lines of the song on a daily basis to deepen your understanding.

☽ ○ ☾

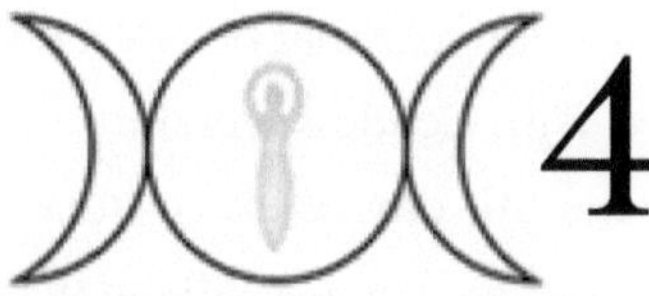

4

Queen and huntress, chaste and fair, / Now the sun is laid to sleep, / Seated in thy silver chair / State in wonted manner keep: / Hesperus entreats thy light, / Goddess excellently bright.

—Ben Johnson[1]

The Maiden Year

This chapter has three goals to conclude our discussion on the celebrating the Maiden Goddess throughout the year. In first section of the chapter, we'll be touching upon the mythic Maiden and exploring what types of celebrations are associated with this. In our second section, we'll be exploring how to craft Goddess-based rituals and prayers to bring a richness to your year in celebration. And finally, we'll conclude with a section on putting it all together—how to craft your own Maiden-Goddess wheel of the year.

The Mythic Maiden

The Mythic Maiden refers to two ways we can approach and craft Maiden holidays (as well as Mother, Crone, and Dark Maiden holidays) during any given yearly cycle. These two approaches are what I call (a) recapitulation rites and (b) mythopoetic-imaginal rites. These approaches may be utilized distinctly or merged together to create a vital and meaningful calendar of rites for you alone or you and your coven. Let's take a closer look at each of these two modes of finding the Mythic Maiden.

A recapitulation yearly cycle is one that is founded upon historical holidays devoted to the celebrations of a Maiden Goddess. In this fashion, you would craft a calendar year that blends a wide range of specific days previously associated with Goddess worship. An example of this process would bee keeping the 6th day of every lunar month (beginning after each New Moon) sacred to Artemis. Athenians also honored Artemis's[2] birth on the 6th day after the New Moon at the end of April or beginning of May, known as festival of *Thargelia.* Yet another festival in honor of her is *Kharisteria,* which was a Thanksgiving celebration. In each of these days, there are specific myths and legends associated with why that day is sacred. Throughout ancient history many deities often had multiple days in the year dedicated to them based on the people's understanding of their mythic history that we can utilize to craft a sacred year. However, a recapitulation calendar is not simply about a literal application of past rituals into the present. In a recapitulated sacred calendar we bring new life and meaning to the ancient rites. In this fashion we look at ways to inject new meaning into the rituals to ensure we are linking to a *living* Goddess energy—not a human cultural past. Recapitulation calendars allow you to build an energy with the past while looking ahead toward the future. These calendars are ideal for covens with specific patron goddesses or which follow a specific cultural tradition; as well as groups that incorporate any form of ancestral worship. These calendars also provide a foundation from which to creatively spring for those of you who are more comfortable with structure and looking to establish a more formalized tradition in the year.

When we consider the Recapitulated Calendar some of the following issues should be considered:

☽ If you are working in a group, it's important not to craft a calendar year that is defined by one mode of Goddess energy. Most members in a group are at different points in their lifecycle or have different energetic and spiritual needs. A recapitulated calendar should readily meet the diverse needs of the members involved.

☽ There's a debate among adherents as to whether one must glean one's spiritual holidays from deities of the same pantheon. I find energy is far more potent when it is based on a match of the spiritual needs of the members and the deity energy invoked. In this fashion, every group needs to make a cohesive decision about which deities and the relationship between them that should be included within a recapitulated or mythopoetic, for that matter, calendar. If you are working alone, having a cohesive idea of what you are seeking is important.

☽ Recapitulation rites have a tendency to become traditional and replicated yearly. They are typically designed to be passed on and give a spiritual path a more religious feel. They also link the present with the past and provide a historical grounded. These are ideal for groups that are carving out their own firm religious tradition that will eventually be hived-off from.

☽ A Maiden Recapitulation calendar can be a beneficial calendar for initiates into a tradition. In other words, in a three-year initiatory cycle, rituals within the first year are structured along the Maiden Recapitulation cycle to match the energy of the rites to the level at which the individuals are coming into the tradition at. These rites may be structured to fall along key elements to be learned within the first year cycle and be further supplemented by other types of ritual structure.

In the mythopoetic-imaginal calendar of the year, the dates and structures of ancient rites are not as important as the myths and your interpretation of them. In this calendar structure, you would craft your own sacred calendar through your reading and interpretation of myths and stories (both modern and ancient) of Maiden Goddess you feel connected to. Through your reading of these myths and stories, you would break them down into seasonal, thematic, or developmental elements and then select days of the year that you feel intuitively links you to these elements. If more than one Maiden Goddess resonates with you consider how the Goddesses relate to each other and to your own needs and locate them in order throughout the year in a meaningful fashion. The key with a mythopoetic-imaginal year is your deepening understanding of the mythic structures as spiritual guides and your own imaginal reinterpretation and retelling of these stories. In this fashion, this is a highly creative and poetic way of crafting a calendar through the year. It is useful if you are in the beginning stages of formulating a tradition—indeed by working with Maiden energy in your beginning stages of crafting, you are further attuned to these beginning steps. Working with this mode of calendar structure can inspire you to elucidate the ethical, mythic, ritual, and energetic elements of your tradition. However, applying this mode of ritual structure to a group that has been working for a time can pose some challenges as the mythopoetic-imaginal element is highly individual and perspective-based. In this situation, it can be a good idea for each participant to retell the mythic stories that speak to them at designated times in the year—in this fashion, each member brings a celebration to the group through their own mythic vision.

☽○☾ Symbol & Ritual Tip

A rich way of bringing Maiden Mythopoetic-Imaginal rites into a Goddess group is to have each member select a Maiden Goddess energy they feel intimately connected to and to choose a day in the year where the group gathers and the member "Witnesses the Maiden", by this they retell the mythic story of the Goddess and Her powers that all members can claim, followed by a ritual created by the individual. If you have first year initiates in your group, this can also be day where they take center-stage and lead their first ritual. Additionally the Mythopoetic-Imaginal rite is one that emphasizes creativity, storytelling empowerment, and performance. This in turn allows members to experience greater spiritual ecstasy as well as helping individuals build a sense of trust and greater confidence in themselves.

☽ ○ ☾

A Word on Rituals & Prayers

Are there any set patterns for a Goddess ritual? No. One of the critical elements of Goddess-based worship is that it emphasizes speaking and acting from the heart—from your core creative and intuitive self. Individual Goddess worship is centrally intimate and spontaneous. If you intend to work in group some simple structure is important to ensure all members can equally participate—more on this in a moment.

When setting up a ritual, it is important to set aside space for this to occur. In antiquity, most devotees and priestess/priests of the Goddess had small shrines (sometimes embedded in their house with larger communal areas set up in mountain sides—grottos). These sacred places of worship contained a statuary of the Goddess and a place for offerings. In some homes a grotto may have contained several Goddesses who were known as the "Household Gods"—ancestors and deities that were patrons of the family. As we develop in our connections to the Goddess, we often find aspects of Her we feel most closely tied to. When we feel this intimate connection, setting up a permanent grotto to Her in your home can be an important step in your year of celebration development. As you move through this book, hopefully by the end you'll have developed a deep and abiding connection with Goddess. And as such, hopefully you'll have an opportunity to set up personal shrines to each of Her aspects, bringing Her totality into your life. So what's in a **Goddess Grotto**[3]?

Visually resonant symbols of the Goddess are always present in a sacred grotto. In Mongolian Shamanism, it is believed that certain objects become houses into which the energy of a deity or ancestral spirit would take up residence. In this fashion, taking time to consider what items serve to represent your deity is important as not only will these representations come to facilitate your ritual transformation of consciousness, but will also come to harbor the sacred energy of your patron Goddess Herself. There are numerous options for you to select from that can act as a sacred house for the Goddess from statues, art prints, to nonhuman symbols. I encourage you to utilize your instinctive, spirit self to help you identify what object feels most right to connect to the goddess. I strongly encourage you to look toward nonhuman symbols as these can often reflect totemic aspects of the Goddess as well as serve to viscerally remind you that the Goddess is not "human" per se, but in all things. I have found that one of the greatest challenges for students is to thealogically recognize the Goddess is not human and that our mythic understanding of Her is human simply because the limitations in our perspective-taking.

In addition to an image to help you connect and focus upon having a small offering dish to practice your devotion to the Goddess is helpful. Any type of dish can be utilized as an offering dish, when I look to refresh my own altars, I often will go to a local dollar store to purchase a unique plate that I feel resonates with the Goddess I am working with. Offerings are our way of showing and performing our sense of gratefulness to the Goddess. They are symbolic acts that reinforce our own sense of gratitude, connection, and participation in the sacred act. What you offer will depend on what you feel most resonates with the energy of the Goddess. I like to offer bird seed and items found in Nature that I can later return to Nature in a ceremony. Others offer small items such as colored ribbons or coins or flowers. Consider the mythos of the Goddesses you are working with to determine which offerings most resonate for you and do not hesitate to listen to your instinctive understanding. When you are new to Goddesscraft it can be tempting to engage in it through formulaic means that this can stifle your growth.

On my altars, I often include a prayer box. I utilize a prayer box to hold my prayers that I am asking the Goddess for help with, affirmations, or spells that I have conducted in association with the energy of the Goddess. I will often place a sacred stone or herbs in the box in keeping with what I have asked, affirmed, or cast. Your prayer box, if you work alone, should not be opened by others. I often consider the prayer box to reflect the cauldron of the altar, where the Goddess and I are symbolically merged; where there is both immanence and eminence.

Candles, incense, and anointing oils are all additional additives that can create a sacred atmosphere, while also serving to help you shift your focus from your mundane life to your spiritual worship. The act of lighting candles is a process of reflective of illumination and can be a wonderful way of beginning your devotion. Incense and oils also serve to affect a shift in consciousness through the sense of smell, while the act of anointing transforms objects into sacred tools. In short, your Goddess altar should always be kept clean, neat, and have items that reflect your own spiritual understanding and support your intimate time with the Goddess.

Once you have your grotto, the question becomes what do you do? As noted in the beginning of this section there is no right or wrong way to honor the deity. Authenticity and love are the only requirements for worship. Many Goddess devotees focus their time at their altar spontaneously giving expression to their Goddess, reciting a prayer that reflects their understanding of their Goddess, singing a song, or in quiet meditation. If you work within Wicca, than you may develop a more elaborate ritual whereby you cast a circle, call the four elements/quarters, before engaging in your work with the Goddess. If you work in a group, then developing shared rituals are important. This can be as simple as using a "call-and-response" chant or prayer, whereby adherents can easily catch on to the leader's inspiration—or it may be developed into a more complex planned ritual, see Appendix B for information on structuring ritual in a group process.

Regardless of how you structure your ritual, the real key is to allow yourself to be spiritually affected by the rituals you participate in with the Goddess. Finally, it's also important to note that you do not need an altar to be able to authentically interact with and worship the Goddess—saying a prayer upon rising or upon eating or upon going to bed can be just as effective. On sacred days, having a special meal can be an equally powerful ritual as with having a focused ritual at an altar. So remember the kinds of prayers or rituals that you wish to engage do not need to be elaborate—just authentic, sincere, open, and loving!

The Maiden Year

You've now had the opportunity to explore Solar, Lunar, and Mythic Maiden Goddesses and it's time to experiment with crafting a Year of the Maiden. Again, there is no right or wrong way to craft your sacred Maiden year. So what are some things to consider in your crafting?

- **Your focus.** First you need to consider how you want your Maiden year to unfold. If you are anticipating a year ahead where you are going to be making changes and seeking to manifest personal growth—then your celebrations should shepherd you along this journey. You might wish to take a developmental cycle or create your own mythic cycle that traces several Maiden Goddesses along your own path of change and growth. In this capacity, your year should affirm (make real) how you wish to grow and change. On the other hand, if your goal is simply to get to know or merge with the Goddess at a more intimate level, then you might wish to create a calendar that honors that Goddess or Goddesses.

- **The Goddess.** Clearly you cannot have a sacred calendar without knowing who you are honoring and working with. We can feel called to one Maiden Goddess or several. They are all aspects of the Divine energy and thus all equally of value. Regardless of how many Maiden Goddesses you feel called toward, you can celebrate them throughout the year. To learn about which Maidens speak most to you—take time to read myths, look at artwork, and look at attributes and meditate—many times the Goddess will literally speak to you.

- **Establishing Sacred Days.** We can craft a range of Holy Days from daily to monthly to only a handful of times a year. If you feel called to only one Maiden Goddess consider creating a sacred day per month in honor of that Goddess that allows you to learn more about Her. Consider giving each of these days a "sacred" name that reflects an element of that Goddess—such as The Day of Athena's Wisdom or the Day of Athena's Might. Optionally, you may wish to honor a different Maiden each month. You may also engage in daily prayer practice with one or several Maidens. Finally, you can follow set calendars (Lunar/Solar) with your own constellation of Maidens who speak to you.

☽ **Goddess Grotto.** Once you've moved through your planning stages you are ready to implement and apply your spiritual goals and your sacred attention by working within a sacred space either individually or collectively. Taking time to craft a space in your life and in your heart to welcome the Maiden Goddess in is critical and is the final step in creating a Maiden Wheel of the Year.

Once you've got your days, grab a calendar (or make one in a creative way) and note them down. I highly recommend obtaining a day planner for the year that allows you to write in it or transform a journal into a day planner. In this not only mark your days, but also begin to journal about your ideas for prayers and rituals. Another activity I recommend is the Goddess Mandala, whereby for each sacred day you create a mandala that reflects the meaning, energy, and Goddess of that day—this can also be the very ritual you engage in as creating Mandalas can be a sacred process itself. You may wish to express these days through other creative means, such as a collage, or a poem. Do this for all your months and hang them up as the time turns toward them. Optionally consider crafting a large paper wheel with your sacred days noted, consider adding a spinner to turn the wheel to highlight your sacred day (think Wheel of Fortune's giant wheel). Be creative and have fun!

☽ ○ ☾

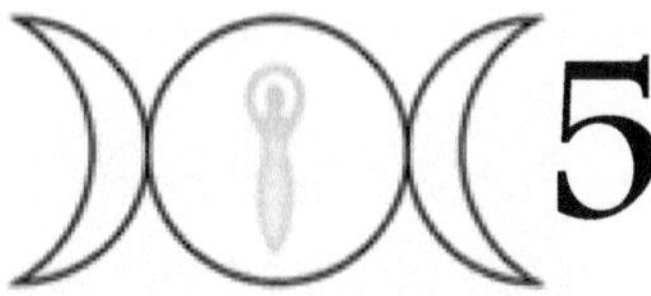

5

I found a fiery, active female and a passive, watery male. The fact of a god of the moon, connected to feminine things like menstruation and fertility, was a bit hard to take. However, he is only the stimulator, while the sun goddess actually experiences pregnancy or bleeding. — Sheena McGrath

The Solar Mother

Before we begin to explore the Solar Mother, we need to take some time to explore what is meant by the *Mother* Goddess. The Mother Goddess is one of the most complex and challenging of the three Divine aspects to understand, largely because She has undergone a wide range of very overt mythic changes over the years.

The Mother Goddess began Her message loud and clear as complete in and of Herself **Creatrix**. She emerged within human consciousness as symbolically seen as the source of All that is, was, and will be. She was the literal center of the universe—a pan-ultimate Divine force who pathogenically birthed the whole of creation. Within Her dwelt all Her aspects—Her past self and beginning, the Maiden; Her present creative self, the Mother; and Her future constraining and diminishing self, the Crone. She had no form, but was heat and energy that stirred the void. She was at once Chaos and Order; Light, Shadows, and Darkness; Nothingness and Something. She was wholeness, neither Male or Female. In the words of Bendis, a Dianic High Priestess:

> We find the idea of "male and female energy" uncomfortable and limiting, and also impossible to define. We view Goddess as Whole, containing all. We also view ourselves as Whole, containing All. I do not need someone, outside of myself to be whole. I do not need another to provide bal-

> ance in my life. I know that I am a blending of all energies, and balanced, just as I am.[1]

Thus the Great Creatrix reflects completeness and the embodiment of all potentialities of life. In this very issue, She ultimately cannot be either male or female, since not all life emerges based on sex divisions. When we consider the Great Creatrix, we are working with the energy of Wholeness, Allness, Oneness, and the Potentiality of Creation[2].

As human culture developed and expanded, the Creatrix became carved into a divided Self (the separation of the Maiden and the Crone from Her, as well as the emergence of the Son and Sage). A Male principle and a Female principle were drawn out, with one set in the sky and the other *grounded* in the Earth. Sky Fathers and Earth Mothers emerged. We catch a glimpse of the Creatrix in Her Wholeness in the remaining Earth and Nature Mothers—the keepers of the *whole* of life and who perpetuate the turning of the seasons and facilitate the growth of plants and the birth of new babies.

In the dividing of the Creatrix, life no longer begins pathogenically, emergent from the very force of itself, rather it is a sexual process—the union of the Male and Female—and we have yet another image of the Mother: the *sister-wife-lover.* She becomes defined as either receptive or subversive. She is Saraswati the loving wife of Brahma and She is Hera the subversive and rebellious wife of Zeus. She is the literal mother of the Gods and Goddesses. She is an image of a heterosexual union, where the roles between men and women are clear and divided. She is Yin to the Male Yang—completeness becomes only synonymous with the merging of opposites.

The Mother aspect of the Goddess is challenging and can be problematic if we focus our gaze to Her mythic emergence within a patriarchal culture. She is defined by her *relationships* to others, generally Her *brother-spouse* and Her children. She is Demeter, a Grain Mother, who can only be fully functional in her relationship to Persephone, her daughter[3]. She is Isis the rescuer of Osiris, the devoted spouse who literally moves through hell to put the pieces of her husband back together.

She is Hera who is often imagined in myth as the wife eternally nagging Her husband and seeking to undermine His authority. These later myths of the Mother Goddess must be carefully explored in relation to what we know about Nature and the biases of culture. In other words, we must challenge ourselves to go beneath the myths passed down to us because they manifest very clear cultural biases that silence the full power of the Mother Goddesses. In this capacity, as you explore the Solar Mothers, the Lunar Mothers, and the Mythic Mothers, it is can be important and liberating to consider the following:

☽ How has the myth denied elements of the Mother's *wholeness* by relating Her power and stories tied to Her spouse or her children? What is denied are the hidden elements of the Mother's power—the Goddess Mystery we can discover and thus return to light a more complete presence of the Divine Mother in our world.

☽ How does the dominance of heterosexism preclude not only the Mother's parthogenic self-creative abilities, but also deny the creative relationships between same-sex couples? We know that sexual orientation in the whole of Nature is highly flexible. What are the hidden elements of the Mother's power (and for that matter even the Male Principle energy) when we consider Her as a sexually free individual? Who is She without a spouse or Her relating to the Spouse?

☽ There is a dominance of myths of the Mother emphasizing Her capacity to give birth and raise child deities—many later myths of the further demoted Divine Mother into an elevated Human status (Virgin Mary), emphasizing self-sacrifice. How might we challenge our understanding of the whole Mother when we consider her as *childless Mother*? What do we find when we seek to see how she is creative outside of child-bearing and rearing? What are the mysteries of the Mother Goddess who exists apart from Her Children—

who is creative unto Herself? How is She creative when She is not procreating?

☽ Finally, rape becomes a mythic element in antiquity and many of the Goddesses become mothers through this act of violence—speaking to the literal erosion of the Goddesses' powers. Spending time to consider these elements in the myth and how may the Goddess's trauma be witnessed can help further illuminate the greater depths of the Mother. This can also be a critical element for women who themselves have been raped to reclaim their own power.

With these questions we come to our role as priestesses/priests[4] of the Goddess, the Great Mother, who intuit and seek beneath the surface of the waters of the cultural myths. Just as mother in our human contemporary culture is loaded with often restrictive messages of how women should be, the Mother Goddess too has suffered from silencing of Her power. She is more than Her relationships; exploring this "more-ness" allows us to deepen our understanding of Her mystery. In other words, when we approach the Mother we want to see out her Wholeness—and this may also mean challenging our own creativity as we re-examine and re-envision the myths that have been passed down to us.

Before concluding this section, we often find the Mother Goddess in five visions: (a) the Whole Creatrix, the Pan-ultimate, the Everything; (b) the Earth Mother; (c) the Parental Mother; and (d) the Sister–Lover–Spouse Mother; and (e) the Artistic Mother. Depending on where you are in your life, you may find that one, all, or a mixture of these aspects resonates for you and what you are working on. You can craft your solar (and lunar and mythic) year to manifest these aspects as you see fit. Briefly consider the following:

☽ Whole Creatrix—this can subsume all other divisions of the Goddess and you may wish to work with this vision if you are focused strictly on the Goddess path (not other Neopagan traditions whereby there is a Male/Female principle). This is an encompassing and complete vision of the divine.

- Earth Mother—Goddesses that are Grain, Ground, Tree, and Earth Mothers can be very beneficial if you are seeking support and insight in coping with cycles of middle-adulthood. This includes times of perimenopause, career changes, launching children, and returning to education, as well as if you are seeking a greater spiritual closeness with the Earth and nature. These deities are often comforting when faced with untreatable chronic or terminal diseases during your middle adulthood or a terminal disease of your child (think Demeter ultimately having to lose her daughter to the underworld and her ensuring winter grief).

- Parental Mothers—these are Goddesses who are specifically associated with their Children (they may function as Earth mothers as well). Their stories are family focused and their energy is directed to home and relationship functioning. If you are a mother or father and struggling with your children or you just need greater insight or support, than these Goddesses can be very helpful.

- The Sister–Spouse–Lover Mother—these are Goddesses who are known specifically in their relationship to their spouses. There are a wide range of Goddesses evidencing both support for coping with and leaving dysfunctional relationships and those who manifest a loving and equal relationship; there are also those Goddesses who manifest magic and healing to literally save their spouses. Often courage and heroinism emerge in the sheer will and strength these Goddesses manifest in journeying to the underworld. These can also be Goddesses to support those of you who are seeking love and to find your soul-mates—after all the Goddesses journey to the underworld to save her spouse is also a shamanic soul-mate journey. Re-imagining the Goddess with sexual and relational flexibility is important here since many myths are constrained by heterosexist values and ideals and do not necessarily reflect the full embodiment of the Goddess.

☽ The Artistic Goddess—many Mother goddesses are also the Goddesses of creativity, such as music, art, poetry, and divine inspiration. This is often a less explored element in myth and one that requires a little creative re-imagining but it demonstrates that to be Mother does not mean to be restricted to solely a procreative position.

A Year of the Solar Mother

In a year of the Solar Mother, we are looking at the development and full manifestation of the Mother Goddess. A year focused on the Mother Goddess enables us to fully capture and explore the many nuances of meaning and energy of this Great Being. In a Goddess developmental-based year, we only capture of glimmer of the Mother as parent and lover, we do not see Her complete self. However, when we focus our year in Her specific celebration we have the opportunity envision the fullness of Her life, not just her belly. Just as mature men and women wish to be seen in totality, rather than functionality, so too does the Mother Goddess. The Goddess of the Solar year is a parent and lover, but She is also artistic even career minded. She is interested in Her own personal growth and reflection, just as She might be in that of another. Let's now turn to a specific discussion of the year.

A Solar Mother Story of Ostara

(March 21 or 23, Western Hemisphere)

The Year of the Solar Mother begins with Ostara, the time of Anna Perenna, the Roman Goddess that reflects the literal ring of the year—the renewal of the year itself. Thus Anna Perenna literally gives birth to the new year and the new potentialities and possibilities of that year. In this fashion, the Solar Mother year begins with the message of creative potentiality.

It is an optimistic beginning about manifesting what one knows, what one is capable of. While the Maiden focuses on developing one's vision and experiencing oneself as complete, the Mother year encourages us to build on what we know. Anna Perenna returns, as She always has—She is not new to the world. She has lived experience and maturity. Yet She is not finished with Her birthing cycle.

When we reach our mothering/fathering age we have years (hopefully) of time spent knowing who we are. We have gathered practical knowledge and perhaps even spiritual knowledge as well. We are no longer "new" to the world, but rather renewed to the world each year. Our developmental focus is on getting our needs met and facilitating the needs of others in our lives. We are not solitary, but embedded within a wide range of relationships, some of which may be romantic or parental. The narcissism of youth has given way to a recognition of our relatedness to the webs of life and our communities.

Anna Perenna is not new, nor is She nearing completion—She has nearly an infinite return—forever in a state of mature possibility and potential. When we begin our Mother Year, we begin the year charged with honoring what we know, growing in what we do not know, and manifesting the range of creative potential that emerges in our own being and within our relationships. Thus we find all of these theme emergent in first days of Spring, when landscapes slowly renew itself. Spring is dominated by the return of vegetation, which ultimately is often the continued expression of the Mother's creative potential. The Mother renews Herself, which paves the way for the introduction of new life.

Solar Mother Mystery Rite for Ostara

Ostara is the time of acknowledging the potentiality of your roots. The

Earth renews itself through the sustained life of the roots that have remained healthy during the cold of the winter. The shoots are not new children per se; they are manifestations of the mother plant. It isn't until blooming and fruiting in the summer and early autumn, does the Mother Plant give birth to new children. For now, the Earth is renewed by the mother's own power. In this fashion, the Mother Rites of Ostara may be explored in the following ways:

☽ Honoring, healing, or breaking from your personal roots—your family-of-origin and your ancestors. The elements that are healthy or unhealthy of your life that has brought you to the current year—this new year. This is a time of breaking ties that inhibit your potential or reawakening your familial resources to manifest your potential.

☽ Knowing your own roots—we all have intellectual, creative, spiritual, and career roots—things we enjoyed or felt called to in our childhood or things we developed skills in but may have forgotten or need to see in a new way. During Ostara we can once more journal and reawaken these feelings and decide how we might manifest them in the world around us—how can we push up shoots of this in the year.

☽ Consider hydroponically growing plants and placing them on your altar so that roots are exposed or consider crafting a celebration meal with root vegetables or transplant a well rooted plant or plant bulbs charged with your own goals for fruition.

A Solar Mother Story of Beltaine

(May 1, Western Hemisphere)

At Beltaine the first flowers have bloomed, the time of Maia—the May Mother of First Blooms; it is a time of attraction. It is the time of Aphrodite, the Goddess of Lovers who not only oversees the flourishing of the flowers, but also the union and joining between individuals. Through our capacity to join with others we are able to manifest our full creative potential, just as the flower awaits the wind or the insects to transmit pollen to fertilize new flowers and perpetuate the species. It is a time of attraction—we are drawn to others. We recognize our own power to bring into the world what we need and to transmit the pollen that will fertilize our dreams and desires. We are both the flower and the bee—contributing holistically to create both honey and a new being. We recognize that in relationships we give and we gain, ideally in equal measure.

Solar Mother Mystery Rites of Beltaine

This is a time of excitement and flourishing. If possible, celebrate outdoors where fresh flowers bloom and insects buzz. Consider incorporating symbols of bees and other insects on an altar and take time to journal about who are the helper insects buzzing around your life. Consider having honey-cakes and mead and celebrate with those in your life who help fertilize your ideas and transmit your goals. If you are in a committed relationship, consider taking time to explore how each of you fertilize or support the creative potential of the other. If you are seeking a relationship take time to identify your relational goals and how you want to be supported—craft a beeswax candle and burn your request to release it to the universe.

A Solar Mother Story of Litha

(June 21–23, Western Hemisphere)

Litha is the High-point of the Mother Solar Year, where Her Solar aspects shine brightest. Litha is the longest day of light the year and the Solar Goddesses reign. It is the day of Surya, Igaehindvo, Walu, and Arinna. This is the day where we contemplate the Mother as the Sun

Goddess—whereby the streams of light are the procreative menstrual blood reenergizing the world. This is the day of fullness whereby the Mother Goddess is unto herself. She is neither wife nor parent—she is in the business of shining and extending her energy. She is a career woman at this high-point of the year. She is the majestic magistrate overseeing the world beneath her. She is illumination and judgment. She is adept at Her work of providing the energetic resources to sustain life.

Solar Mother Mystery Rite for Litha

This is the time of year to honor your work and your sense of purpose. If you are unclear of how to merge your sense of purpose with your work/career, now's the time to shine a light on it. Consider crafting a ritual to allow the universe to shine a path on the best type of career or work for you.

If you are working to sustain your children or your partner, this is an ideal ritual to celebrate yourself. We often do not take time out of our working for others to give ourselves a period of rejuvenation. This is the ideal time for us to give thanks to ourselves. It can be a time to also honor your own mothers and fathers who have worked to provide you with the resources you need. We can use this day to thank those around us for providing us our resources that help sustain us, just as we also honor and thank our own beings for our own capacity to manifest resources. If you are a single parent working tirelessly to ensure the well-being of your children, this is a day to honor your work and replenish yourself. Taking time to commune with the Sun Goddesses can allow you to find a literal renewal of your energy and to feel yourself cared for by a being greater than you, just as you provide this sensation to your children.

☽ ○ ☾

A Solar Mother Story of Lammas

(August 1, Western Hemisphere)

Lammas has two Mother meanings. It is a day that highlights the Mother as significant other. In Celtic traditions this is often associated with the Marriage of Lugh, a Celtic Vegetation God. In Goddess traditions we may think of this as the day of Frigg, Saraswati, Hera, Rhea, or Metis sacred wives of Sky Gods and Titans. There is a Goddess for all types of relationships—just as many men and women are in romantic relationships that are struggling, harmonious, or outright unhealthy. This is a day when our relationships with significant others—and our relational styles and patterns of engagement—take center stage. It is a time of gaining wisdom into our relationships and what is needed.

This is also a time of the first grains and as such it is also a day of the Grain Mothers. Demeter, Ceres, and Corn Mother are all invoked on this day as corn and wheat ripen and are readied to sustain us through the coming winter. In this fashion, this may be seen as another "career" day of the Goddess. We find her manifesting Her divine job of providing food. While Litha showed Her providing pure energy to sustain life, at Lammas She is the nourisher of Life.

Solar Mother Mystery Rites of Lammas

As there are two meanings of this sacred day, we can work with it in unique ways. If we are in a committed relationship, we can explore a Goddess that reflects how we'd like the relationship to unfold. If it is a dysfunctional relationship, we might wish to work with a more subversive Goddess to help us reclaim our power and reshape the relationship or leave it. As this is also a nourisher day, it also reminds us that relationships are the "food of life" and thus if they are starving us or making us "sick" than we need to change them.

As this is also the day of the Grain Goddesses, it is a time to look at how we nourish ourselves and how we nourish others. While Litha encouraged us to shine a light on our purpose and our skills and what we do, this is a day to shine a light on how we do things. What do we literally and metaphorically bring to the table and is it sustaining to others? What do we contribute to the world around us and how do we do it? You may wish to buy a fresh piece of corn and peal it back and as you do so gradually peal away the layers of who you are to uncover a core element of yourself—a literal kernel of wisdom!

A Solar Mother Story of Mabon

(September 21–23, Western Hemisphere)

At Mabon we arrive to the day of the First Fruits. It is a time in Nature when the fruits have reached their fullness and start to fall from the vines and trees. This is the Mother birthing the world. In this capacity we encounter the elements of the Mother goddess as her role of procreator, progenitor, and Great Nurturer. The fruits are Her seed that is ready to land on the energized and fertile ground. This is the time of the Gift-Giving Mother Gefjon. It is the time of Idun, whose apples symbolize eternal life and the ever-present cycle of fertility. It is the time of Parvati and Lakshmi who nourish the world with compassion, benevolence and rejuvenation.

Solar Mother Mystery Rites of Mabon

At this time, we slow down and appreciate our labors and the work of others. We look for ways to give ourselves and extend ourselves to others. We understand ourselves as nurturers. It is a time of looking at how we will foster the next generation and celebrating with them. It is also a time of looking at what we are leaving the next generation, as such this is an ideal time to consider environmental issues and participating in planting or clean-up projects or making commitments to change how you address the environment.

☽ ○ ☾

A Solar Mother Story of Samhain

(October 21, Western Hemisphere)

Samhain is a time when the many complex facets of the Mother emerge where we see the richness of Her personality unfold. We may see Her strength, destructive, warrior abilities, and ability to cut through bull in her manifestation of Oya, Sekhmet and Durga. It is a time when the Mother may take a journal of self-discovery braving the underworld such as Ishtar and Larunda. It is also a time when the Mother loses their child and grieves over the loss, such as Nanna. It is a time of chaos for the Mother, where She must dig into Her depths to tap into resources of self—She no longer has children or a spouse to define her. She is in a time of chaos and upheaval. The routines of Her life are at an end. This is the perimenopause of Her life. She is at the precipice of change and transformation.

Solar Mother Mystery Rites of Samhain

The mysteries of Samhain are diverse depending on your transformational needs. This can be a day of empowerment and releasing anger. It can be a time of undoing old patterns and behaviors and taking a risk to redefine yourself. It can be a time of healing grief and healing from relational loss (break-ups and divorces, for example). It can be a time of also promoting health during perimenopause stage for women. In this fashion, Samhain is a private time in the Mother year. It is a time of solitary experiences and going inward. It is a time of fleshing out who you are and not being content with being one-dimensional. If you've been pigeon-holed into a way of being, this is a time of finding your depth—fleshing out your deeper self.

☽ ○ ☾

A Solar Mother Story of Yule

(December 21–23, Western Hemisphere)

Yule is a time of the resurrecting Mother. At Samhain, She lost her Lover. At Yule, She harnesses her re-creative and rebirthing capacities. She is Isis and Cybele. She embodies magick and ingenuity, patience and persistence. She is a healer and a miracle/wonder worker.

She is also the embodiment of hope. When all light is lost and barely visible, the Great Mother is able to flourish. This is a Mother who has the capacity also for self-regeneration. She has weathered the chaos of Samhain and has found herself anew. She is once more prepared to share her newfound self with the world.

Solar Mother Mystery Rite for Yule

Yule is a time where we can celebrate our ingenuity, our survival strengths, and our capacity to recreate ourselves and the circumstances of our lives. If events in our life need overhauling, now is the time for us to tap into our resiliency, creative problem-solving strengths, and our magickal selves to transform them. Even in the darkness, we are capable. The Yule Mothers remind us we can survive chaos and come out transformed for the better—they also remind us of our transforming effect on others. We may also use this time of the year to engage in forgiveness rituals and other rituals that allow us to move on and forward with our lives. If a relationship is floundering, this may be the perfect time of year to get a clear picture of it and where you want it to go. It is a miracle season where we can become and be anything—where our own mystery, our own hidden powers, can be revealed.

A Solar Mother Story of Imbolc

(February 1 or 2, Western Hemisphere)

Imbolc marks the last day of the Mother Solar Wheel. The year ends at

Imbolc and in the end we encounter the primal Mother. The enduring light behind all life—the enduring nourisher. It is a time of the Great Cow Goddesses: Damona, Hathor, Hera, Adhumla, Sechat-Hor, Tailtiu. The Goddesses who nourish life behind the scenes, the foster mothers and mothers alike who stand behind and allow their children to unfold and flourish and begin the overt light. It is the Dawn Mothers, such as Máter Matúta, who shepherds the rise of her Maiden Sun daughter.

Solar Mother Mystery Rite for Imbolc

At Imbolc, we see how we support and stand behind others and those who in turn are behind us. At Imbolc, we set aside our ego to light the way for others. It is a time to let others shine. It is a time for us to honor the successes of others and to appreciate how we are not the center of the universe. At the Mother's Imbolc, consider celebrating the success of those in your live—whether they are coworkers, friends, significant others, students, or children. As we celebrate others we in turn become aware of how the Great Mother, in her Wholeness and her Primordial self, stood back and admired creation and felt that it was all Good.

☽ ○ ☾

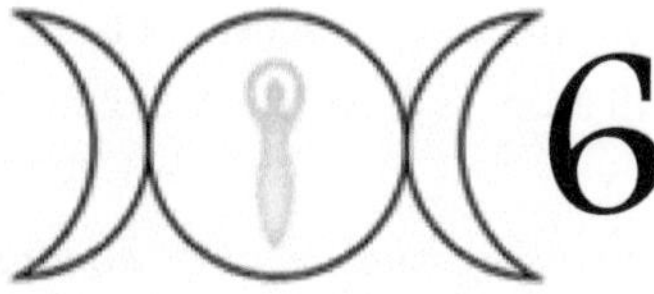

6

Once all have been the center of the circle,
the leader opens a jar of white face paint,
turns to the woman beside her and
paints a full moon on her forehead, saying
"White Moon's blessing shines through you tonight."
The leader blesses each woman with this tangible sign
and then leads the group in the mantra:
"I am the moon, the moon am I,"
conducting the beat of the mantra by
drumming a simple rhythm at different tempos.
— Nancy Brady Cunningham

The Lunar Mother

The Lunar-Mother Wheel

Previously we explored the Lunar cycle by the first crescent moon before the full moon (optionally you can utilize the first quarter) as a symbol of the Bright Maiden. In this chapter, we are looking at the Lunar Mother as She manifests within the Full Moon or the pregnant moon. Nancy Brady Cunningham refers to these moons as the moons of "shining magic"[1], demonstrating the general property of this moon as a working moon for spiritual and personal development. Indeed, the full moon reflects the generative and procreative powers of the Mother Goddess, whereby the fullness is reflective of imminent birth. It is a time of potent and highly accessible energy. Z Budapest writes:

> When the Full Moon comes around, go out dancing, no matter if it's a weekend or not. Take note of your energy

> level. You will find you are active till late at night and not tired. The Full Moon is good only for ritual, lovemaking, or dancing.[2]

She further notes repressing one's energy during the Full Moon can lead to disruption, chaos, and irrationality. I would also add that this is a time when we experience the Goddess's own dramatic cosmic hormonal changes as she delivers the world anew—and if we are not prepared to funnel this energy into nurturing ourselves, others, and our personal goals and desires—we can experience emotional upheaval. As children of the Great Mother, we too are being asked to fledge—to leave her womb; to jump from the nest; and to risk development, growth and maturity. The Full Moon is the time when we have an opportunity to rebirth ourselves, begin again, and recommit ourselves to our personal growth, vision, and relationships.

The Maiden Moons are times of untamed action, passion, impulse, instinct, and experiencing. They are times of anticipation and daydreaming and of looking ahead at what is to come. They are moons of youthful optimism and throwing oneself, body and soul, into one's life. They are moons of experimentation and exploration and discovery. As such, they are Moons of being uncommitted—of being open to any path and opportunity that presents themselves.

When we encounter the Full Moon, we are committed. We are preparing to nurture what is coming into our lives—what we are giving birth to. This is a moon where we are no longer single so to speak. Instead, this is a moon where we can focus on our actual relationships and strengthening, recommitting to, or refining them. Yet, also this is a moon where our desires and personal goals and aspirations become our children—our babies that we are charged with caring for. In a sense we are being charged with the goal of nurturing our own beings—bringing ourselves safely into maturity, bringing all we hope for into the full blossom of life. For example, you may wish to make a substantial career change—during the Full Moon, you can direct energy into this goal so that it flourishes and takes off. It moves from the position of the Maiden

☽ ○ ☾

Dream, into actuality—into fruition (literally fruiting or giving birth). Hence the Full Moons are the times of shining magic—visible, glaring, overt, clear, illuminating, and fully manifested actions. Full Moons are the time when we can take charge of our lives and direct the extra Moon energy we experience toward our goals, dreams, and desires.

As with the Bright Maiden–Lunar wheel, each Full Moon is an opportunity to experience and direct a different type of energy. Z. Budapest breaks these times into three primary elements that create each Lunation (a moon month): Moontale, Moontide, and Moonspell[3]. In brief (we'll expand on these elements shortly)[4]:

☽ **Moontale** refers to the words of the Goddess associated with each moon and also reflects one's internal processing and meaning-making of this Goddess. Thus it is the story of a Goddess and it is your own personal Moon story as a manifestation of the Goddess. Within Goddess traditions, the Goddess dwells within us—we are Goddess (often referred to as "Thou Art Goddess")—and without us. The Goddess dwells independent of us. In this capacity, we encounter the Full Moon as both goddess and in celebration of The Mother Goddess.

☽ **Moontide** refers to the emotional component of the Moon—how the Moon impacts our sense of feeling; the ebb and flow of our moods, dreams, and desires. The Moontide reflects the element of change, both subtle and dramatic, that we engage in. It also reflects our relational selves as we are drawn toward and away from others.

☽○☾ Symbol & Ritual Tip

These three elements can also be utilized within all other phases of the Moon, such as a Bright Maiden Moontale, Moontide, and Moonspell; a Dark Maiden Moontale, Moontide, and Moonspell; and a Crone Moontale, Moontide, and Moonspell.

☽ ○ ☾

☽ **Moonspell** refers to what type of work is supported by the specific Moon we are in. It is the how we direct the increased energy of the Moon during its fullness. It is the shining magic we engage in.

Crafting the Lunar-Mother Wheel: Moontale

The Moontale has two elements: (a) the Words of the Goddess of the Lunation and (b) your own personal story of the Lunation. Within Goddess -based traditions, we are all the priest/esses of the Goddess and we are all capable of hearing and speaking Her story. Each Full Moon—the marker of the month—provides a time for us to intuit and reflect on the full meaning of the Great Mother as She manifests during the month in Nature and in our lives. In this fashion, when we identify a Goddess for a particular Full Moon, taking time to allow Her to speak through you and tell you Her tale can be a rewarding way to deepen your understanding of the Moon. Moontales can emerge through poetry, re-visioning myths, channeled writings (such as the Sybils of the past have done), or re-reading myths already written. Your Goddess Moontale can be as creative and elaborate as you'd like or simple. If you work with others during the Full Moon celebration, having each member become a conduit for the Goddess of the Moon story and share their vision can be as rewarding as any work.

Yet, the Moontale is not simply the tale of the Goddess Without. The Moontale is also your own personal tale of how the message and meaning of the Full Moon speaks to you. This is the tale of the Goddess Within. Taking time on the Full Moon to journal about personal experiences in your life that reflect the energy of the specific Full Moon can provide you with greater insight and meaning. Your own personal Moontale allows you to see how the Goddess's energy dwells within you and manifests through you. For example, if Isis is one of your Full Moon

Patron Goddesses, then your own Moontale might look at your own resiliency, dedication, capacity to problem solve, or your courage to pursue and protect those and that which you love.

☽○☾ **Symbol & Ritual Tip**

In the shamanic path of Voodoo, they interpret the middle world (Earth) as emerging in two locales that interrelate with each other and seek to balance each other, the Marketplace (human culture/society) and Nature. This is a useful way of fleshing out the Goddess in that She speaks to both our cultural sensibilities and needs, as well as manifests in fullness in Nature. Thus, She dwells both in the Marketplace (the artifacts of our human life and experience in culture) and in Nature. Reflecting on both of these aspects through a Moontale can be a rich and rewarding experience. Optionally, you may also consider your own personal Moontale to be reflective of the Marketplace, while the Mother Goddess' Moontale is reflective of Nature.

Finally, another way to look at the Moontale is to tell the tale of the Marketplace and Nature—in other words to see how the Goddess manifests in these unique and often opposed areas. How might the Goddess unite them together? How does the Goddess of the Full Moon bridge the divide between Nature and Human Culture? How, in turn, might we too bridge this divide? This is a particularly beneficial type of Moontale for our current experiences whereby human cultures is imperiling the natural world. How might the Goddess bridge these ever-widening divides?

Moontales can become a rich center point to a communal meeting in celebration of the Full Moon. The act of storytelling is as ancient as our capacity to speak and is the foundation for all religious traditions. Thus when we gather to tell our Moontales we are all reinvigorating and tapping into our primal religious and spiritual impulses and contributing to the ongoing revelation of faith and the presence of the Divine in our lives.

Crafting the Lunar-Mother Wheel: Moontide

Myths down through history have linked the Full Moon with our emotions and having the power to transform our encultured selves into animal beings. Folklore and urban legends have informed us that Full Moons are times when our primal emotions, our basic instincts, our core beings and passions are unleashed. In this fashion, Full Moons are times of transformations with each Moon bringing to shore a different sense of being.

The Moontide is the emotional tide of the Full Moon—what it awakens in us; how we feel about the world, ourselves, and others around us. For those who engage in more shamanic-based Goddess craft, the Moontide is also how we shapeshift—shift our perceptions and energies into another type of being; merging our energy with another animal dwelling in the world with us. Thus the Moontide is a time of sensing and feeling the world through another perspective—the boundaries that divide us humans from other living beings blurs. We can literally shift our emotional and perceptive selves into another being—we remember that within us contains the potential for all other living beings and vice versa. Genetic traits sleeping for the time being, waiting for the next tide of evolution to awaken them and transform us into who we may become next. As such, the Moontide puts our rational, pragmatic, and rigid side of ourselves on hold. It challenges us to expand our understanding of reality and linear time. It is a time of blurring the edges of the photo, much like the ocean waves break unevenly and never in the same place and never in a straight line. The sand shifts in unpredictable, random ways under our feet as the tide pulls out—ever-reshaping the landscape

☽ ○ ☾

in subtle but distinctly different ways each time. The Moontide is about that type of perception—the perception of the fractals, the uneven shapes in life, the seeming chaos, the softening edges.

Each Moontide will be experienced emotionally and intuitively. Our rational minds may seek to define it and solidify it, but the Moontide cannot be predicted. It is immediate and present. It is not past, nor future. It is NOW. While each Full Moon may have a unique direction or meaning, the Moontide will inevitably change. Discovering your personal Moontide—how the Full Moon makes you feel and how this influences and reshapes how you see the world and your life can be a powerful way of not only informing your Moonspell, but also expanding your sense of how the Goddess is communicating to you. You are the sandy shore, the coastline, and the Goddess is rushing up to transform you and shape you with her ever-present and constant tides. Yet despite the constancy, the tides are ever-changing, ever-challenging; thus each Full Moon asks us to reflect on what we feel and how we are being transformed right now. I generally recommend you avoid reading books telling you what the emotion is you should feel and dig in to develop a relationship with each Full Moon to understand what the Goddess is communicating to you in your present, immediate moment.

Crafting the Lunar-Mother Wheel: Moonspell

The Moonspell is what you do with the energy of the Full Moon that has come upon you. Once you know the tale of the Goddess within and without and once you sense your tide, you can determine just what type of energy you have and how this matches with your goals, dreams, and desires. Whether you follow a more witchcraft-based tradition that directly employs magic or not, the Full Moon Moonspell is about growth and manifestation. No other moon phase is as potently connected to having energy to direct outward in specific ways. The Bright and Dark

☽ ○ ☾

Maiden Moonspells tend to be short-term and often less specific; while the Crone Moonspells tend to be reflective and introspective. But the Mother Moonspells, the Moonspells of the Full Moon, look toward long-term manifestations and bring important goals into fruition. They are Moonspells that look to affirm (make solid) elements of ourselves that we are ready to commit to. For example, a Bright Maiden Moonspell might look to deploying energy to try something new, such as take a chance with a glass blowing class. In contrast, the Mother Moonspell would seek deploy energy to design a series of glass art—a more sustained and directed creative endeavor.

Crafting Moonspells may be done in groups, with shared energy focused toward issues that individuals have in common for that Moon phase[4]. Your Moonspell may be as elaborate or as simple as your group calls for. Or you can work privately to craft a Moonspell that most suits your current needs.

> **☽○☾ Symbol & Ritual Tip**
> Many of the Solar Mother Goddesses are also Lunar Mothers, such as Isis for example. In this fashion, there are a lot of options in terms of crafting a Lunar-based Mother Goddess Wheel. Some additional goddesses that are related to the Moon you might like to explore[5]:
> Atargatis, Hina, Ixchel, Chang-O/Chang-E/Heng-O, Coyolxauhqui, Mut, Mawu, Sirdu/A, Juno

Native American Moons & the Mother

☽ Wolf or Old Moon (January): This is the Full Moon of the Mother Goddess who has launched Her children and stands at the new precipice of what She will nurture now. She sits at the transition between fertility and menopause. She is the Wolf Mother who has successfully brought to age the next generation of pups. This Mother Moon all about taking time to reflect on the moment of stillness—when we have completed one nurturing/creative/procreative task and are awaiting the next impulse to generate. It is the Full Moon reflecting on the iced-over, still lake.

☽ Snow or Hunger Moon (February): This is Full Moon Mother of yearning. It is the moon where we begin to feel pulled toward a direction, away from the stillness of the prior moon. We feel an intuitive urgency, a building drive and pull. This is the moon where we begin to crave something new and feel the first inklings as to what that new project will be—whether it is related to career, personal goals, self-development, or relationship. During this time, we take the first steps to literally "feed" ourselves with what will eventually help nourish our later goals. It is the first trimester of pregnancy, before any overt changes have occurred. Your goals and desires for creativity and expansion and birth are still your own to keep secret as you need. Your actions are still invisible to the outer world—the work you put into yourself and your goals in this stage, however has long-term consequences. Feed yourself right.

☽ Worm, Crow, Crust, or Sap Moon (March): This is the Moon Mother of announcing—of signaling the shift from stillness to rebirth. It is a time when your goals begin to "show"—the second trimester of renewed life for the Mother. The ice is melting and the waters are unfreezing, reminding us that this is a time of overcoming the barriers that might inhibit us—of allowing ourselves to go with the flow and break out of rigidity. During this time, we become more fully aware of our goals and more fully embodied by them. We look at taking more direct steps toward manifestation. We may address aspects of our lives that are more obvious or clear, but which need nurturing and support. We move more purposefully and consciously toward our goals. We may also feel more anxiety during

☽ ○ ☾

this period of time as we become more conscious of what we want and more committed to it. Thus this is a time of also quelling our fears and reminding ourselves to relax and trust ourselves.

☽ Pink, Sprouting, Fish, or Egg Moon (April): This is the Full Moon Mother of the third trimester. We are fully pregnant and showing—we cannot deny our goals and purpose, we are fully committed to this process. We are now anticipating the manifestation of what we have put in place. During this Moon, we can contemplate our capacity for completion and fruition. We often focus our energy on the failed or unfilled projects and dreams (the miscarriages of our lives), but this is a Moon that reminds us to focus on what we have brought to term—to look at our lives more completely and to honor our capacity to commit and stick to our goals.

☽ Flower, Corn Planting, or Milk Moon (May): This is the Full Moon Mother of birth and infancy. We have given birth to our goals, but the work is not done. We must feed our goals. They are no longer an internal part of ourselves, some secret seed kept deep inside us, but they are now visible and taking on a life of their own within the universe. It is our job to feed them—they are not fully independent of us. This is the formative stage of our goals and dreams. We must feed them with kind words, compassion, and love. We must shelter them from those that would undermine our success or provide us with negative energy. This is the time of building positive energy and support for ourselves and our goals.

☽ Strawberry or Rose Moon (June): This is the Full Moon Mother of young childhood. It is a time of joyfulness and exploration. The sweetest fruits have emerged and the world is alive with the fullness of spring. It is a time of discovery and excitement of seeing the world anew. It is a time of stepping back on our self-protectiveness to allow ourselves to fully embody our goals and to test the renewed

☽ ○ ☾

image of ourselves in the world around us. It is a time of letting ourselves come out to play in wonderment and openness and to experiment with where we our in terms of our goals—to see where we need to develop and move into. We are at once Mother and Child.

☽ Buck, Thunder, or Hay Moon (July): This is the Full Moon Mother that allows us to regroup. As with all children testing the world around them, we too in our goals will fall down and bruise our egos. Not all our goals will manifest flawlessly or perfectly or in just the way we'd like. Occasionally we must weather a storm and upheaval. This is the Full Moon that allows us to reassess and strengthen and heal ourselves. It is a moon that reminds us to get back up and try again. It reminds us that we are imperfect and through our imperfections we learn. This is a time to appreciate our bumps and bruises and scars—to remind ourselves of our capacity for resiliency.

☽ Sturgeon, Green Corn, or Grain Moon (August): This is the Full Moon Mother watching over adolescents. It is the high-heat of summer and passion. The Mother Goddess not only directs Her energy to Her growing children, but also rediscovers Her own passion anew. The Moon Mother looks to fulfill Her own relational needs, just as She seeks to nurture all her children. This is the time when we may feel torn between our commitments and need help in balancing our energy so we do burn out. During this Moon we may look to ensuring that we balance our caring of others with our caring of ourselves. Our goals often take a backseat as other relationships come to the forefront—this is the Moon that allows us to work through these potential conflicts so that we don't lose our enthusiasm for our own needs and self-commitments.

☽ Harvest Moon (September): This is the Full Moon Mother of Abundance and Prosperity. All the work of the Great Mother has become fully manifested in the world around us. All the Children have been born and reached maturity—adolescents are now adults and the Great Mother can sit back and look at how the world has matured and developed and anticipate the possibilities that are embedded within each creation. We are part of these creations and within us are the seeds of the Goddess—we are Her fruit that has ripened on the vine and drops to reseed the earth and spread Her energy outward. At this Moon we must appreciate and take stock of our Divine Seed within us. Our goals and dreams are not simply products of whimsy, but a reflection of the impulse of the Goddess in our lives, speaking to us.

☽ Hunter's Moon (October): This is the Full Moon Mother of initiation and action. We have the last burst of energy before winter quiets us. This is the Moon of the Mother as the sustainer of Her children and people. She is the Great Huntress, the Fisherwoman, and the Goddess of the Wilds. She is the Great Mother Bear preparing a den to give birth in during the cold months. During this Moon, we assess what we need for the coming cold—the coming time of stillness.

☽ Beaver or Frosty Moon (November): This is the Full Moon Mother of the first month of the winter season. The Mother Goddess is receding from the landscape. We encounter the story of Demeter, whose Daughter has returned to the underworld, leaving Her Mother alone. This is the Mother who grieves for Her losses. We have all experienced some loss in our lives—this is the Moon to heal our grief from breakups, deaths, divorces, and even our children growing up and moving on. This is the moon to heal from failed dreams and the endpoints in our lives, when we have to change our goals because of physical, emotional, or financial changes in our lives.

☽ Cold or Long Nights Moon (December): This Full Moon Mother is but a shadow of Herself now. She has receded from the world to replenish herself. This is a time of inward reflection and self growth. She experiences her aloneness completely here. She is neither mother nor wife nor sister. She is unto herself. She is sleeping and dreaming. This is the time for us to take a moment to see ourselves independent of all others—to dig in and see who we are and have become.

Celtic Tree Moons & the Mother

☽ Birch (12/24–next New Moon): As this is the moon of inception this is the moon that signifies conception and the beginnings of pursuits, goals, and dreams. The Mother Goddess is seeded with new life and waiting to bring this into the world. Specifically she is seeded with the light of her indwelling son/sun that she will soon birth back into the world.

☽ Rowan (January): This is the moon of vision and the Great Mother is growing full with her pending birth. We are each full of the growing sun--the abundant energy that we will be able unleash toward our life. This is the time of nurturing that growing internal sunlight and to make preparations for how you would like see the coming year unfold.

☽ Ash (February): This is the quickening moon and the moon of floods—the Great Mother has given birth to the sun. This is the moon where we may set into motion a goal for the coming year. Our energy is at its peak and ready to be deployed.

☽ Alder (March): This is the moon of utility and the practical—this is the Mother Goddess who concerns herself with the hearth and home. This moon is about identifying what you need to get your goals in place.

☽ ○ ☾

☽ Willow (April): To counterbalance Her practical goals, the Moon Mother during the Month of Willow is a time to counterbalance the prior month's seriousness. The Moon Mother engages in her creative and enjoyable activities at this time. She reminds us to balance our energy and be sure to not only nurture others, but to nurture yourself as well.

☽ Hawthorn (May): This is the moon of temperance and patience. The Moon Mother does not unleash Her creativity all in one fell swoop. She paces Herself, just as we should. This is the moon for us to remember to slow down and pace ourselves as we manifest our goals. She reminds us to pay attention to where we are in the moment and engage in moderation.

☽ Oak (June): Like the Great Oak, this is the Moon of Strength. This is the Moon Mother of Isis and Cybele who continue forward despite the loss of their husbands. They are the widowed Mothers who continue forward as beacons of optimism and hope. This is the time when we must remind ourselves of our inner light and strength. The Goddess dwells within us and as such we have access to her Strength. This is a moon of commitment to our journey and our goals.

☽ Holly (July): As the Moon Mother arrives within this moon She seeks unity and closeness and intimacy. She is no longer the Widowed Mother, but the Mother who has once more merged with Her lover. This is the moon that reminds us to recognize we are not alone, but share our journeys with others. She reminds us to seek closeness and intimacy with others—to be able to share our unique, authentic selves with others.

☽ Hazel (August): This Mother Moon is a wisdom moon—we are

asked to reflect upon the totality of the Mother Goddess and Her wisdom. This is a moon where we contemplate how her fertility has manifested in our lives and in the world around us.

☽ Vine (September): As the lunar year turns, the Moon Mother enters into the period of exhilaration and excitement. This is a time of renewed and abundant energy. The Mother is not withholding—She extends herself outward and as such, this is a moon of sharing our energy and our successes.

☽ Ivy (October): This is the turn of the year as we move from the warming, blossoming months to the cold and withering months. It is the moon of balance. The Mother Goddess stands at a transition between fertility and barrenness. This is a time of reflecting on how we all move through cycles of fertility and sterility and that such cycles are beneficial and balancing. We do not have to always be generating, doing, creating, procreating—we can be fulfilled in the absence of these actions.

☽ Reed (11/1–11/26): As the seasons turn, the world actively seeks to prepare for winter. This is a time when we look to securing ourselves. This is the Mother Goddess who provides for us and reminds us to take an honest look at how we provide for ourselves. It is a time of also working on moonspells that seek to ensure our security (emotionally, physically, and materially).

☽ Elder (11/27–12/23): This is the culminating Moon of the Celtic year and I would generally say that as a moon of completion this is a moon of the Mother Goddess as Creatrix. This is the Moon Mother in Her completeness. This is the time when we honor our fullness. This is also the time of the good-enough mother—where we understand ourselves good enough in our lives.

☽ ○ ☾

The Coligny Calendar & the Mother

While the Celtic Tree Calendar is disputed by most scholars as little more than an invention by Robert Graves, the Coligny Calendar discovered on several tablets and corroborated historical literature does appear to reflect another structure of time keeping that could be adapted by a modern Goddess adherent. This is not to say that Robert Graves ideas and intuitions are not appropriate to apply, indeed religion should never be stagnant but reflect an ongoing revelation of the divine. The Coligny is a lunar calendar that mediated between a solar and lunar mode of organizing time; it's believed that ever 2½ years it added an extra month. Below is the assumed structure and meaning of the calendar based on Caitlin Matthew's work,[6] the specific translations of the names of the months are still obscure.

☽ Samonios (October/November), the "Seed-Fall": Within this cycle of time the focus is on preparation for the future. In this cycle, we look toward the Mothers who shepherd us toward the future. We look in our ritual cycles as preparatory ones—shaping our energy, psychological state, our spiritual, and our cultural goals toward setting the stage for future growth. We shed our seeds—that which we have fertilized and are ready to sit back and watch grow. We look toward the pregnant Mothers for this energy.

☽ Dumannios (November/December), the "Darkest-Depths": This is a time of journeying downward and inward. It is a time of psychology and spiritual mystery and deepening awareness. We may experience challenges in our emotional and personal lives that force us to dwell in the dark. The Mother goddess of this time are those who dwell in the dark places—those who have had to journey to the underworld to reclaim what has been lost and to restore balance and light. This is a time when we must journey below and find a way to live within the shadows and the darkness.

☽ Riuros (December/January), the "Cold-Time": Appropriate for the Northern Hemisphere's coldest winter, when all things freeze, this is a time when there is little movement. This is the beginning of a longer period of rest and indwelling. This is a time when the Ice Mothers rule—when the beautiful Snow Queens dwell in the land challenging all who live to find their peace, their nourishment, and their rest. During this time, we are asked to contemplate our lives as they are frozen in the now. It asks us to find peace with the things that we cannot change, the situations that only time can eventually alter. This is a time of reflection of what elements of our lives are not in our control.

☽ Anagantios (January/February), "Hibernation-Time": All beings need rest—a time when dreams become the dominant source of reality and the other-realms are journeyed to. In our natural landscapes, living more closely toward Nature, this is a time when we stay in more frequently. When our outer-self gives way to introspection and altered states of consciousness. While our modern technological age forces us to continuously interact, our natural energy drive in this time is introverted and often lower. This is a time of the Ursa, the Great Mother Bear; it is a time of the Mothers who nourish our interior worlds. It is a time of following the dream and the journey—of stillness and innerlife.

☽ Ogronios (February/March), "Time of Ice": In preparation for Spring, the land freezes, gathering up the moisture of the Winter snows and stilling the waters. This is a time of getting things prepared—the first hints of spring emerge and we begin to feel the first internal stirrings to get back out into the world beyond. This is about the beginning steps, preparing for the year to come. We look toward the Mothers who are preparing for the quickening.

☽ Cutios (March/April), "Time of Winds": Winds are necessary to pollinate and the winds of March signal the changing of the climate—warmer temperatures mix with cooler ones and storms and wind emerge. It is the turbulent time of the Quickening. It is the time of rising energy and optimism and possibility. We are prepared to enter into the world anew and bring something with us. This is the time of the birth itself.

☽ Giamonios (April/May), "Shoots-Show": Life returns to the landscape and the Mothers have birthed their Divine Children; they are reunited with their children. We are in the active presence of the creative power of the Mother and in turn can direct this toward other elements in our lives.

☽ Simivisonios (May/June), "Time of Brightness": Life is vibrant and growing under the nourishment of the Mother. We are fed by the Spring and our energy is at its highest point. We can look toward how to flourish and shine in where we are.

☽ Equos (June/July), "Horse-Time": This is a time of movement and of exuberance. We are directing our energy outward toward our goals and our ideas. We honor the Mothers of Movement, Swiftness, and Decision.

☽ Elembiuos (July/August), "Claim-time": This is a time when we commit and dedicate ourselves toward our goals, our relationships, and our ideas. We claim our rights and we empower ourselves. We honor the Mothers of Marriage and Art and Nature—those who have dedicated themselves toward another.

☽ ○ ☾

- ☽ Edrinios (August/September), "Arbitration-Time": This is a time of atonement, forgiveness, and settling disputes. It is a time for negotiation and letting go. We look toward the Mothers of Compassion and Wisdom during this time to allow us to "see" clearly and to free ourselves from that which has been toxic in our lives, as well as make amends for our own mistakes in ways that allow our energy to be freed.

- ☽ Cantlos (September/October), "Song-Time": After a year of work and introspection and dreaming, we reward ourselves with celebration and song. This is a time of creativity and memory, of eulogizing and celebrating, all things end but in the ending we can celebrate the journey. We look toward the mothers of Loss and Muses, of the turning of the time and of fate.

The Coligny Calendar provides another wheel around which to turn in your year. It is applicable to Maiden, Mother, or Crone energy and can be easily adapted to fit the developmental movement of all three of these energies. I encourage you to explore this mode of time if you are living in the Northern Hemisphere. If you are in the Southern Hemisphere, just adjust the months to your seasonal cycles.

☽ ○ ☾

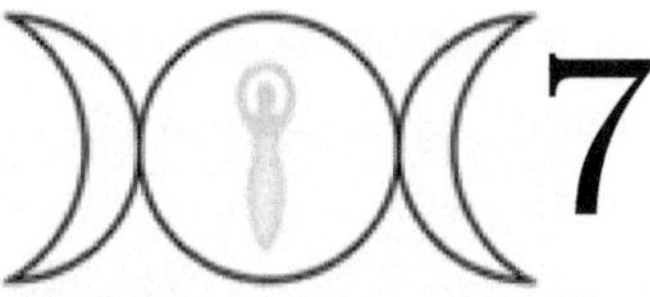

7

And now, queen of the land of sweet Eleusis
and sea-girt Paros and rocky Antron,
lady, giver of good gifts, bringer of seasons, queen Deo,
be gracious, you and your daughter all beauteous Persephone,
and for my song grant me heart-cheering substance.
And now I will remember you and another song also.
–"Hymn to Demeter", Homer

The Mother Year

The Mythic Mother

> Fixing the distant origins of Great Goddess worship in the female's ability to reproduce is biological reductionism at its most pernicious. This has been one of the major ways in which women worldwide have been stereotypes, devaluing all of our other human traits, and it does not take into account the varied contributions of women to culture, including those who cannot or choose not to reproduce. While childbirth probably was seen as awesome in cultures in which paternity was unknown, as was women's periodic bleeding without dying from it in cultures that did not connect menstruation and maternity, to suggest that those physiological functions alone accounted for the supremacy of the Great Goddess is to beg the question of whether there is ever anything new under the sun.[1]

The Great Mother Goddess is more than the biological function of a mother—defined solely by her capacity to give birth and her capacity to literally engage in act of mothering. The Great Mother Goddess cannot be rigidly confined into our internal ideals of what constitutes a "good mother" and "bad mother"—a division we've often seen in fairy tales of the Good Witch and the Bad Witch or the Virginal Mother and the Whore. The Mythic Mother Goddess demands more from us. She demands our capacity to fully realize the breadth, depth, and mystery of Female energy and force—of shakti[2]. As such, when we encounter the Mother aspect of the Goddess, we are encountering the Goddess at the midpoint of Her energy cycle. For all women and men who are in their thirties through fifties, chances are what defines these years is not child-rearing alone, rather it is about defining one's sense of self through one's actions, clarifying one's productive and creative goals, developing and sustaining meaningful relationships—and then perhaps caring for children. In this fashion, when we encounter the Great Goddess in Her own midlife, we are being asked to know Her with the same search for depth of purpose and meaning we ourselves experience in this stage of our own lifecycle.

We can dive into Her depths through the specific contemporary and ancient celebrations dedicated to aspects of Her being we are drawn to. As in our earlier chapter of the Maiden Year, we can explore the Great Mother Goddess as she was celebrated throughout the year worldwide through Recapitulation. We may take the month of June, for example and dedicate it to the discovering of the fullness of Juno—the Mother of the Young Gods. We may direct our attention to contemporary Goddess -worshipping cultures, such as Hinduism. Kathleen Erndl writes:

> The worship of Devi (the Goddess) is one of the most vigorous and visible of religious phenomena in northwest India....She is worshipped in a variety of forms and manifestations and enshrined in temples....each is considered to be a manifestation of shakti.[3]

In Asia, the Mother Goddess is alive and flourishing in yearly celebrations that have been passed down continuously for thousands of years. In this fashion, we can craft a Mother Year that draws upon the sacred days of the ancient past or the present. Days which allow us to craft a year of celebrations enable us to explore the depths of this Midpoint Goddess. And through this exploration, we also come to flesh out our own complexities and discover our own edges where we blur into our younger selves and anticipate our older selves.

The Mythic Mother Year is also a year of the here and now. The Mother may be seen as the mystery of the present moment—She is the Now of our awareness; while Her Maiden Self is then and Her Crone Self is coming. The year of ritual and prayer within the context of the Mother is one of manifesting immediate fullness—knowing who we are completely in the moment; learning to appreciate our full beingness. The myths of the Mother and Her associated celebrations down through history can become vehicles for this process of growth and awareness, that by the end of our mythic year we are thus re-birthed to ourselves—we come to a new understanding of who we are and our relationship to the Divine world around us. In this we may work within a mythopoetic-imaginative structure as we create a new story—a story of immediacy and revelation—within the year.

Mother of the West, Mother of the East: A New Story

Understanding the Mythic Mother is not complete until we also understand the two faces of the Great Mother as She manifests in our contemporary time. While antiquity saw the Great Mother as a critical figure throughout the world; a central focus of worship both within the domestic and within the public spheres of life. She was at once a force of Nature, as She was a force of Culture. In antiquity, Her mythos was shared between cultures—while there were important differences, they were often subtle and never obscuring the face of the Goddess as a unified whole. Now Her continuity, completeness and unified self has changed—She is split. She is a double-faced Goddess.

Like the myth of Janus, who looked to the future with one face and to the past with the other, the Great Mother Goddess, too has sprung two heads. One looks toward the past, a continuous vision of Herself, unchanging and unconquered from the Paleolithic. Where She rises in the East—preserved in the faiths of Hinduism and Buddhism and manifested as the Female Principle of Taoism. But Her face of the West is mutable. She has been transformed from the bountiful, force of life into a pale vision of Herself. She has been denied Her outright divinity and power—a shadow of Her former self as Her voice creeps through Western consciousness as the Virgin Mary, the Jewish Shekhinah, Saint Brigid... She is no longer Creatrix; Her power diminished and humanized. She has become the "weaker" sex, the secondary being, the mother who sacrifices herself for all others. She has identity only through Her sacrificial or maternal functions—She has been suppressed.

Joining with and working with the Great Mother requires us to come to terms with Her contemporary duality. We are asked to locate and explore our own splits in our lives. Where are we torn between Nature and Culture, between East and West, between individualistic and collectivistic ideals, between our outer and inner natures, between self and Other, between mind and body, between thought and emotion. As we explore our Mythic Mother's split, we seek to restore Her wholeness and through this act we too become complete—we are full and we encompass all things.

As we examine the mythic year, we can consider the Goddess of the West as the Winter Goddess, the one who has lost so much of Her luster in the face of spiritual and philosophical erosion. She is the petrified statue of history, who stares at us from the marble statue—frozen in time. This is the Mother of the West. During the winter and fall months of the year we may consider crafting a new story of this denied Mother—coloring in the pallid statues and restoring the vibrancy and meaning of Her beingness. As the wheel of the year turns we many look to Spring and Summer as the time of the Eastern Mother. The Mother who is richly defined—whose presence remains visceral and whose worship has never been halted. She is the Lady of the Gilt, richly maintained. Crafting our year that allows us to restore the Great Mother to Her Global Self gives us a new vision of Sacred Womaness. We reclaim and restore the Mother to Her spiritual truth. We tell a new story.

The Mother Year

When we come to feel connected to the Great Cosmic Mother, we can determine how we will honor Her throughout the year and thus honor ourselves. As noted in the two prior chapters, we might do this through the traditional solar calendar or a lunar one. Or we might craft our year based on ancient sacred days associated with the Mothers. Or we can craft our own—new days to reflect our new relationships with the Great Mother. Mythopoetic-imaginative traditions to bring Her presence back into the world around us. Some ideas to enrich and inspire your Mother Year:

☽ Consider celebrating the Mother in Her modern dual aspects—with a Summer ritual on the Solstice celebrating Her sustained self—Her powerful energy that remains visceral within the Eastern cultures. Then on the Winter Solstice, consider reclaiming Her Western power—the Divine Mother of God where Mary becomes Ma, the Great ancient Mother. Incorporate symbols of the East and the fiery passions of Lakshmi—with lotuses and rich fragrant incense. At the Winter solstice, consider the statue of the Pieta, whereby Mary was sculpted to dominate the image—Her large hands and encompassing body as She holds the "dying sun", the diminishing "light of the world", consider white lilies and other flowers to illustrate Her own creative power and capacity to bring forth the Light—to hold fixed the cycles of Nature—thus to dive deeply into the now hidden face of the Western Goddess—who has no husband, who is the creative force unto Herself.

☽ Consider each Full Moon as a time of sacred mystery—of diving into the depths of the unknown Mother. Each full moon becomes a time when we can explore Her fullness and thus our own.

☽ Consider the rising and the setting of the sun as a time for the celebration of the Mother. She births the world anew in the morning and during this time we can see ourselves as renewed. She dies and returns to Herself at dusk, where She will dwell in mystery of the coming dark. It is a time when we can encounter our hidden depths.

☽ Finally, consider your own key moments of your midlife—take time to identify critical turning point moments of this time, such as committing to a relationship, leaving a long-term relationship, childbirth, child-fledging (sending children off to school for the first time and then to college or into their own independent lives), committing to a career, etc. Consider each of these turning points and place them at moments in your year—find the Mother Goddesses that speak to you for each of these events and develop a ritual celebrating your own growth!

☽ ○ ☾

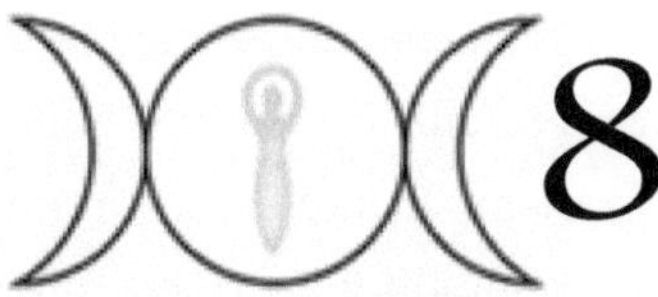

8

The Crone was the most powerful of the Goddess's three personae. Seen in myth after myth as an old woman, she was yet stronger than any god. Under one of her Teutonic names, Elli or "Old Age", in a wrestling match she conquered even the god of strength, Thor himself.

—Barbara G. Walker

The Crone

The Crone is a figure of great power and depth. She has walked the world an eternity over and is a giantess of wisdom. The Crone remains at the edges of Western Consciousness as that which we fear: the Hag who carries children aloft in the dead of night, who haunts the dark roads, and lives in the battered and abandoned buildings. She is the awesome presence of death and resurrection and the inevitable. She is Skuld; She is necessity. She reflects that which human life continuously fears: old age, desiccation, endings. She is the turning of the year where life withers, hibernates, and the wind howls. She is the shriek against the shutters and the Nightmare. She is the power of the uncompromising force. She is the Tribal Elder. She is the future of each of us, just as She is often the rejected, masked, and hidden self we become. We cover Her mark upon us—in an attempt to ward Her presence off, rather than embracing the power She brings to us.

The Crone IS.

We become enfeebled when we resist Her power and sway. We become withered, when we reject Her wisdom. We become childlike when we forgo Her strength and independence. We weep when we stand at the gates of Her house when we look backward at what was and fail to honor what is. The Crone is the inevitable force that pulls us forward in our lives. She is ever-present, not simply visible at the end. She is the drag upon us as we swim in the ocean, reminding us to swim with strength and wisdom; reminding us to live our lives with responsibility, magic, empowerment and a health ego. She reminds us that our lives are gifts, blessed by Her at our birth and taken by Her at our death. She is the Sacred Godmother, just as She is the fearful Hag. She is the beauty that lies within Chaos—giving us the opportunity to change and become our greater selves.

When we craft a Crone Year, we are crafting a year that is transformative. It is a year that allows us to heal woundings; to grieve and transform our grief. It is a year to re-examine the seeming intractable elements of ourselves and re-configure them; re-inspire ourselves into new ways of being. It is a time of shedding shallow vestiges of our being and to dive into our depths and risk the undertow. It is also a time to laugh at ourselves and to take a longer vision of our lives—to put things into perspective and refocus our energy toward what matters most to us. It is a time to free our femininity from the Geisha's shoes—allowing all our lumps, bumps, rolls, wrinkles, and other society-labeled imperfections to unfurl and be celebrated. The Crone year is the year of the Empowered Woman, the Transformed Woman, the Woman who is of no other. It is also a year where we look for opportunities to mentor other women; to support them in their self-expression.

The Crone Year is a year of magic and mystery. Our concentration is not on preparing for a future of the Maiden or on the maintenance of the Mother, but a year of diving into magic and power. The Crone is Magic: a spell-caster, a charm-maker, a prophet, a runecaster, a Seiðr, a cunningwoman, a witch, a healer, a blesser, a midwife, and a hexer. A Crone Year is a year of reshaping, bending reality. She is a wryd-walker—a direct figure of the world tree, standing between three worlds: the middle, upper, and lower world. She is the tree that holds the world together, the Axis Mundi.

☽ ○ ☾

A Crone Year is one that craves the mythopoetic-imaginal structure—demanding we put our wisdom to work. It calls for us to trust our instinct and apply what we know, allowing Her energy to inspire us and our capacity to transform a mundane year into a rich, imaginative, spiritually alive one. I encourage each of you to consider spending at least one year in Crone Worship.

The Solar Crone

A way to explore a Solar Crone year is to understand the Crone in Her eight sacred aspects, many of which overlap within goddesses.

☽ Crone of Wisdom—this is perhaps one of the most recognized aspects of the Crone and one we typically associate with the Crone, where age brings wisdom. She is Hokmah, the Hebrew co-creator and source of "maternal wisdom". As the Crone of Wisdom she is the giver of laws, the dealer of justice, and the keeper of the peace. She is the source of knowledge, both rational/pragmatic and intuitive. She is the Divine Mid-Wife and the source of healing power and knowledge. She is the Old Woman of the Black Stone of Mecca, known as Al-Lat. She is also the Gorgon Medusa, the terrifying daughter of Metis, covered in the symbols of wisdom—snakes, with the capacity to transform those who look directly upon Her to stone[1]. We seek out the Crone of Wisdom, when we are looking for deeper awareness of self, seeking justice in our lives, and accessing healing energy and power. As with all Crones Energy, it contains a seed of defensive destruction—like Medusa who can curse any who would seek to harm her and from whom, whose blood creates and gives life of the magical flying horses (an ancient symbol of shamanic power and wisdom). Crone Wisdom allows us to stand up against oppression. We can honor the Crone of Wisdom at Imbolc (February 2), when the dim light returns to the land and we are asked to commit ourselves to our search for wisdom.

☽ The Crone of Chaos—the Crone of Chaos, from whom the world began. She is the unruly force, without plan or direction. She is formless, shapeless, and ancient. She is asymmetrical and uneven. She is ragged and raging, pulsating and vibrant. She is Tiamet, Khaos, Eris, the Snake Goddess. She cannot be confined. We seek Her out to gain comfort in the chaos of our own lives, the elements of our lives that are not predictable. She reminds us that from Chaos, from the primordial undifferentiated mixture comes life. When we learn to live with the chaos, we can find new brilliant ideas and give birth to a new self. We can honor the Crone of Chaos at Ostara (Spring Equinox), when the Earth is in a state of extreme flux. The weather is wild and unpredictable. A renewed living world doesn't yet know if its coming or going as Winter winds and Spring rains coexist.

☽ Transformational Crone—this is the Crone who contains within Her the capacity to transform life from one form into another, from one state of being into another. This is Cerridwen and her transformational cauldron. This is Crone who resides as the Lady of the Lake and the keeper of the Grail. While her Sister-Self of Time takes life, the Transformational Crone has the capacity to control the cycles of death and rebirth. She is the Immortal and the Magical, within Her cauldron she stores Her "Wise Blood"[2]. She is the Sisters Wyrd, who shape the world in their magical cauldron; She is Kali stirring Her cauldron of Soma (her own fountain of menstrual blood that was seen as capable of invigorating life energy). The cauldron is also Badb, the Celtic Goddess known as the "Boiling One" or Kali who is at once known as the "Ocean of Blood", both are themselves the Cauldron. We seek out the Transformational Crone when we are in need of regeneration—when we need to make a profound change. We become the Cauldron when we take difficult situations and transform them into opportunities for growth and change. The Transformational Crone may be honored at Beltaine (May 1) when the Earth is lush with renewed life. The nourishing blood of the Crone spills into the land from our many fountains.

☽ Shamanic Crone—this is the Crone who travels between the worlds. Hekate is an example of the shamanic Crone, who freely travels between the Lower (Underworld, Land of the Dead), the Middle World (Earth), and the Upper World (the Heavens). She is the wise one who understands the whole of existence. She is capable of lighting the way for all spiritual journeys. She is the "Torch" or eternal light that moves through all realms and may also be seen as the World Tree Herself—the ancient Creatrix who holds together the created universe. We seek out the ancient Shamanic Crone when we are seeking spiritual insight, mystical growth, and seeking a deep vision of our soul's purpose and drive. We may honor the Shamanic Crone on the day of greatest light (Litha, Summer Solstice)—where the Torch She extends is visible and shines brightly in the universe. This is a day of journey work and where we may travel readily between the dimensional spaces of the universe. In Celtic lore, it is often believed this is the day when the faery folk are present and thus capable of tricking us to follow them if we are not careful. Thus we need the shaman's guide to help us negotiate the unique intersections of time and space.

☽ Witch Crone—this is the Crone who is the keeper of magic. She is the guardian of the Wicce, the wise women and men who follow the path of magic. She is also the scientist, for She fully understands the principles of how life operates and magic is situated within this principles. She is also the Crone of artists, poets, singers, writers. She is Saga, Herself—the guardian of the epics to whom all give offerings. She may be seen as the shaper of vision. We may seek out the Witch Crone when we are seeking clearer vision for our creative selves; when we engage in magical work; when we seek to understand the processes of Nature; and when we seek to affirm a new direction in our lives. Summer reaches its last month—the grains are abundant and food is harvested for the colder months. We may honor the Witch Crone on August 1 (Lammas). We are energized by the warmth of the lowering sun and the shifting of seasons. Now as we stand between Summer and Winter, we can gather into us the power of magic.

☽ Hag Crone—this may be seen as the shadow Crone, the first aspect of Her more potent and terrifying self. She is Old Age as a destroyer. She is the terrifying wind that screams death is coming. She is fear of death itself. She is the Warning of the risks of being alive. She is the Wild Woman who dwells in the woods, no longer concerned with what she should be. She no longer concerns Herself with the stereotypes of femaleness. She haunts our consciousness and sings to us on the winter wind. We deeply fear the Hag, who has become immortalized in fairy tales as the witch in the woods, the woman who steels children at night. It is the Hag Crone, whom we turn to during our profound grief. She is the succor for the unexpected losses—when life has taken a violent turn. We may turn to the Hag when we must access a strength within to be our own unique selves and to live authentic lives. We are moving into the autumn of our year, the colder months are coming, and the wind is starting to rise once more. The leaves are turning and the last vestiges of warmth are fading. There is a chill in the air and perhaps a smell of woodsmoke emerges. We honor the Hag Crone at this time (Mabon, Fall Equinox)—She looms over us, reminding us to get our house in order in preparation for the coming cold.

☽ The Destroyer of Worlds—this is the Crone of the End. The Crone who can consume all of existence. She is the end of all worlds, not simply life. She is a Death Goddess of epic proportions. Within Her is the uncreative capacity—the one who resets Time. She consumes the world back into Her yoni, all things return back to her gaping womb. The Destroyer Crone is a potent force that we honor through our own humility—a recognition that while we are a part of life, we are not in charge of life. This is also the Cursing Crone, the one who condemns all of life to its end. She is at the beginning and so shall She be at the end. We seek out the Destroyer Crone when we feel we are at our end—our emotional reserves are gone—and we need a dramatic change and an opportunity to start again. We may also seek out the Destroyer Crone when we are faced with a terminal illness and need Her help to make our transition. At Samhain (October 31), we encounter the Crone in Her Destroyer aspect. This is a day of experiencing our full power and being able to direct it toward our goals. It is a day of re-creating ourselves anew and making a dramatic change in our lives.

☽ Crone of Time—one of the earliest representations of the Crone, what has empowered her to sit above all other Gods and Goddesses, is Her power over time and age. She is the often seen as the last fate, overseeing the end of each life. As noted in the opening quote, the Crone of Time is unmatched by all other forces in the universe, as Walker writes "Old age indeed weakens the strongest, and death indeed conquers even the greatest".[3] In this aspect, the Crone of Time is the goddess associated with supreme fate and the direction of the broad courses of living beings. While Her mothering aspect brings life into existence, the Crone is destiny of all life—She is the unavoidable, the necessity. She is Atropos, Nemesis, Skuld, and Morgan the Fate (Morgan Le Fay). We all encounter this Crone and this Crone becomes a part of each of us. When we honor this Crone we are honoring the force of time in our lives and the shadow of death that ensures we live. Time reminds us of transience and the importance of valuing where we are in the moment. The Crone of Time stands ahead of us and inevitable, reminding us that we have a place to return to, as well as providing us an opportunity to look more clearly at where we are to ensure we are making the most of our time on Earth. A year passes at Yule (Winter Solstice); it is a time of lowest light. We are aware of the passage of time and our own aging process. While the light is diming, reminding us that we are humbled before the force of time, we are nevertheless given hope that even though we age and though death is our ever-present shadow, we have the capacity for hope and continued growth.

The Lunar Crone

A year within the Lunar Crone is one of mystery, prophecy, divination, and transformation. Whichever calendar you select for your Lunar Crone Year, each Lunar month is a month of shamanistic power. As the Moon fades into the New Moon or if you consider the Crone Moon the dark moon itself, it is a moon about the transformative passage into the other realms. The Crone stands between the worlds and during our Lunar Crone rites, we too become the walker between the worlds. One way to consider breaking down this process is as follows:

☽ Autumnal Lunar Rites (September, October, November Moons): The Crone Lunar Year begins in the Fall, when the landscape stands between life and death. We look toward the Lunar rites during the months of the fall and lessoning light as encompassing divination and modes of linkage with the dead. This is a time when we become aware of how the other realms of existence merge with and shape our own. Our perspectives of reality become more mutable and we willingly experience ourselves as standing at the threshold between body and spirit. Healing rites as well as rituals to facilitate a loved-one's transition to the other side are also supported during this time.

☽ Winter Lunar Rites (December, January, February Moons): This is

☽ ○ ☾

the dreaming time when the Crone's feet stand firmly on the other side; when the life of the body stands still and the landscape is encased with a temporary sleep. This is a time of journeying and exploring the landscapes of the other realm. It is the time of mystery, when the living processes of the Earth occur beneath our awareness. It is a time of prophecy and teasing out future patterns based on linking to the energy that flows beneath the surface. It is a time of purging the spirit of negative energy in preparation for the coming spring and return.

☽ Spring Lunar Rites (March, April, May Moons): This is a time when the Crone welcomes and blesses the babes. It is a time our rites focus on blessings and welcoming. It is a time when we look toward generosity and embracing the meaning of Fairy GodMother. We look toward rites of wisdom and empowerment and self-acceptance. We look at rites where we shed ourselves of old habits and ways of doing and embrace the new. This is also a time when we might look at becoming involved in transforming the cultural landscape that undermines women and girl's health and wellness with unrealistic standards of beauty. We look toward bring the truth of Beauty as one that embraces difference, asymmetry, and imperfection to the cultural landscape.

☽ Summer Lunar Rites (June, July, August Moons): This is a time of preparation. The sun reaches its zenith signaling the Crone's descent with the fading light. This is our time to transform ourselves and our rites look at accepting endings and identifying sources of change. It is a time of letting go. Our rites are joyous and embracive of the changes that come. We accept our descent, much like Hecate chose to descend into the underworld with Persephone. This is a good time for initiation for new Crones as they prepare for their own descent into the murky, wise, and mysterious power of the Crone.

☽ ○ ☾

However you choose to craft your Crone Rites, be daring and vibrant. The Crone is uncompromising, proud, and powerful. Celebrating Her allows each of us to embrace our core selves and to experience our inner strength. These are rites that allow us to raise our self-esteem and feel a new independence that needs no one, that seeks to prove itself to none. We are able to stand triumphant in our trust of ourselves. The Crone stands at the gate between this world and the next—She is the equalizer for each of us. She reminds us that our lives are precious gifts and that we can enjoy them and flourish.

☽ ○ ☾

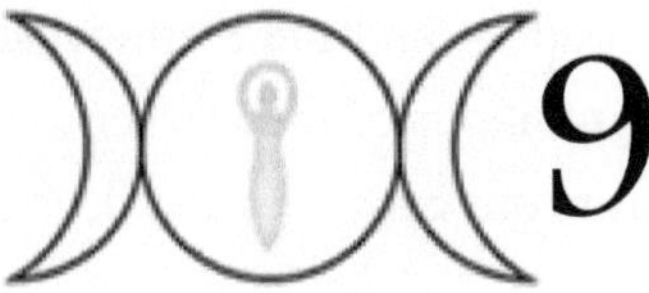

9

I first learned about this Goddess from a lover,
who used to call me her dark maiden,
and point out the waning crescent in the late night sky—
She would explain that there are two crescents and
two Maidens; the Bight Maiden corresponding to the waxing
moon, curving toward the right.
The Dark Maiden corresponds to the waning crescent,
curving toward the left. In older mythic systems,
these maidens can be seen on the labyris or double-bladed ax,
once used by Amazons as a tool and weapon
—Shekhinah Mountainwater

The Dark Goddess

Three Images of the Dark Goddess

The Dark Goddess, as Shekhinah Mountainwater[1] notes in the opening quote, is associated with the waning crescent moon that emerges after the full moon and leading in the New Moon[2]. The Dark Goddess is not a figure widely explored in traditional Goddess thealogy that prefers the more succinct triple Goddess form; however if we pattern our yearly celebration along the moons, then we must account for the waning moon that falls opposite the Maiden's waxing moon. It is here that we encounter the Dark Goddess—emerging in the growing darkness of the night where light is becoming a more precious and limited commodity. This is a Goddess who cannot be solar in nature—this is the Goddess of what is hidden and mysterious. In Goddess thealogy, there are three ways in which we can conceptualize and celebrate this Goddess: the Dark

Maiden, the Dark Goddess, and the Slothwoman. These are three conceptualizations and intuitions of the Darker and Diminishing One have specific connotations to our own lives and development.

The Dark Maiden

The Dark Maiden is most vividly described by Shekhinah Mountainwater, who states:

> The Dark Maiden who wanes…is associated with aging, descent, introspection, and magic. The Dark maiden is the enchantress, She Who Pulls. In Her positive attributes She represents some of the lost powers of woman.[3]

To Mountainwater, the Dark Maiden can be both Crone and Maiden. She is deities such as Persephone, who is pulled down into the underworld and must face the unknown of Her life. She is Atargatis, the Queen of the Mermaids, who draws men down to Her depths at sea and who responds to the tugging and pull of the Moon on Her glassy waters. She is Ariadne, who provides the sacred thread to ensure that we are led through and out of the labyrinth. She is the mystical priestess who dedicates Her life to exploring and diving into the mysteries of the Sacred Feminine.

Mountainwater felt that our Dark Maiden aspects are the most distorted of all our female powers in that we are conditioned toward weakness, passivity, self-sacrifice, victimization, and emotional volatile. To her the "afflicted" Dark Maiden in us is the one who is demonized by patriarchal systems as moody and incapable of positive and affirming action. This is the Goddess often labeled "PMSing" or "hysterical" and "dysphoric". This is the Goddess aspect of women's lives whereby society deems them unwell because of their feminine nature. This is the Goddess whereby menstrual cycles become sources of disgust, shame, and embarrassment. In short, this is both our creative–reproductive selves and the Goddess that reflects all our hidden feminine potential. This is our intuitive, psychic self who typically remains silent in a world that values the Sun, Solar, and the Bright–White. This is the aspects of ourselves that are intimate and often a carefully guarded secret.

When we choose to honor the Dark Maiden at the waning crescent, we are choosing to open up what is mysterious and hidden within ourselves into the world. We are choosing to allow what is in our depths to touch the world around us. When we work with the Dark Maidens—those never-have-been-married women of the Labyrinths, the Forests, the Caves, the Sea, and the Underworld (such as Artemis, Ariadne, Sedna, Persephone, Hekate, etc.)—we are allowing ourselves to encounter our deepest cores, our capacity to shape the world and our destiny, and our capacity to reclaim that which has been silenced in us. The Dark Maiden is the Goddess that opens an unseen road in our lives that reminds us of our capacity for strength and our ability to "see"[4] in the dark.

The Dark Goddess

Demetra George[5] merges the Dark Maiden with the Crone and situates her discussion of the Dark Goddess as one that emerges at the New Moon. In George's model, the Dark Goddess is both creator/transformer and destroyer. She is the demonized feminine aspect in society that has imagined her as a monster who consumes. She has been misinterpreted as finality and something to be feared and destroyed. She is the stayed Tiamat; the transformed and monstrous Medusa; the demonic manifestation of Lilith; the bloody Kali. She is the "Terrible Mother, "the Death-Bearing Crone"[6]. George suggests these are harmful distortions that undermine the power of the Dark Goddess to transform. These are stories that are cut-off and mangled to deny the transformative power of the Dark Goddess to create life from death and to regenerate. The Dark Goddess is:

☽ She is labyrinthine (Labyris); a mystery

- ☽ She is the Unconscious, that which is Hidden in ourselves
- ☽ She is Intuition, knowledge that is hidden and instinctive
- ☽ She is Regeneration following Desiccation
- ☽ She is Cyclical and Predictable in equal parts as She is Chaos
- ☽ She is Life and Death-Bringer
- ☽ She is adept at Healing, Magic and Midwifery
- ☽ She journeys through the worlds as only She knows the structure of the cosmos for the cosmos is born from her
- ☽ She is suppressed, hidden power
- ☽ Her symbol is the Serpent who sheds its skin, renewing itself.

This Dark Goddess can be honored at the New Moon or Waning Crescent. This Dark Goddess is the Women associated with destruction, death, rebirth, and creation. They are the awesome—literally awe-inspiring—All-Women.

The Slothwoman

The final Dark Goddess we will be looking at is known as the Slothwoman. Z Budapest writes of this woman:

> My theory is that deep within ourselves, there lives a creature I call Slothwoman. She is our ancestral brain that is the repository for all our racial memories, that controls, healing; a sturdy creature, to be sure, but speechless. She is into the elements, this brain: fire, water, and earth. She controls our instinctive behavior. Our sex life would be boring without her help and generally she is what we deny in ourselves in this modern life.
>
> In order to impress our Slothwoman, we have to do tricks, like making up little rhymes, easy ones she can rock to back and forth, and make a pretty little altar that would turn her on. We use candles and incense to fascinate her within—use magic, which is her language, her form.[7]

☽ ○ ☾

While Budapest does not develop this image into a Goddess, her intuitive sense of this internal self is clearly aligned with the Dark Maiden and the Dark Goddess descriptions. The central difference is that Budapest has described the Goddess-Immanent—that is the divine She within us. In this capacity, deep within us we have the Goddess Slothwoman; She who waits beneath the surface waiting for us to look for her.

In this fashion, when we awaken the Slothwoman Goddess, She Who Dwells Within, we awaken our divine potential. We call forth from us our Sacred Feminine power—the powers of the Dark Goddess. If we honor, this primal and first self within us at the waning crescent moon, we are seeking to awaken directly our own power. Budapest suggests that this is best awakened by rhythm, spells, magic, creative altars. This deep, hidden and powerful sleeping Serpent-Within is awakened by play, music, creative power, humor, sex, and joy. This draws out our sleeping Giantess from the depths and caves beneath and within. Consistent connection to our inwardly divine Slothwoman Goddess are rituals that ultimately seek to affirm our own power directly—they are rituals that remind us that we are Divine.

Selecting Your Dark Goddess

Determining which Dark Goddess aspect you will ultimately honor and engage within a ritual depends first and foremost on your intuitive sense. The Dark Goddess speaks through instinct, symbol, impressions, and will literally physically pull you toward the mode and concept of honoring. You may find that all three aspects merge into one ritual; you may uncover the dark aspects of a traditionally "solar" Goddess. You may find that your Slothwoman Self mirrors a Goddess—perhaps you have a Hekate Slothwoman within you or a Kali Sloth or a Cerridwen Sloth. The key is to trust yourself and your internal instincts in diving into this mystery. This is a relationship with the Goddess energy that is deeply personal, mysterious, and sacred. This is a creative relationship and so you should allow yourself to engage in creative and spontaneous rituals.

☽ ○ ☾

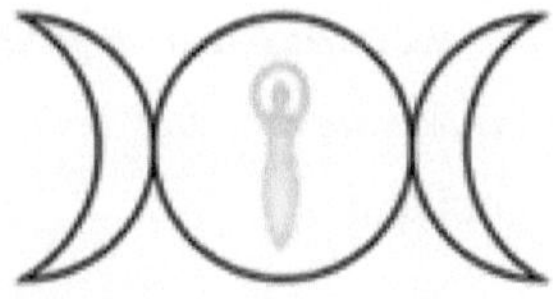

Appendix A

For Further Reading

Barrett, R. (2007). *Women's rites, women's mysteries: Intuitive ritual creation.* St. Paul, MN: Llewellyn Publication.

Budapest, Z. (2003). *The holy book of women's mysteries.* San Francisco, CA: Weiser Books. (Original publication 1980).

__ (1989). *Grandmother of time: A woman's book of celebrations, spells, and sacred objects for every month of the year.* New York: HarperCollins Publishers.

__ (1991). *Grandmother moon: Lunar magic in our lives.* San Francisco: HarperCollins Publishers.

__ (2007). *Summoning the fates: A guide to destiny and sacred transformation.* St. Paul, MN: Llewellyn Publication.

Conway, D.J. (1994). *Maiden, mother, crone: Myth & reality of the triple goddess.* St. Paul, MN: Llewellyn Publications.

Cunningham, N. B. (1995). *I am woman by rite: A book of women's rituals.* San Francisco, CA: Weiser Books.

Downing, C. (1994). *Long journey home: Revisioning the myth of Demeter and Persephone for our time.* Boston, MA: Shambhala Publications, Inc.

Gadon, E. W. (1989). *The once and future goddess: A sweeping visual chronicle of the sacred female and her reemergence in the cult.* New York: HarperCollins Publishers.

George, D. (1992). *Mysteries of the dark moon: The healing power of the dark goddess.* New York: HarperCollins Publishers.

Glass-Koentop, P. (1991). *Year of moons, seasons of trees: Mysteries & rites of Celtic tree magic.* St. Paul, MN: Llewellyn Publications.

Graves, R. (1966). *The white goddess: A historical grammar of poetic myth.* NY: Farrar, Straus, and Giroux

Lubell, W. M. (1994). *The metamorphosis of Baubo: Myths of woman's sexual energy.* Nashville, TN: Vanderbilt University Press.

King, K. L. (1997). *Women and goddess traditions: In antiquity and today.* Minneapolis, MN: Fortress Press.

Monaghan, P. (1999). *The goddess path: Myths, invocations, and rituals.* St. Paul, MN: Llewellyn Publications.

__ (1999). *The goddess companion: Daily meditations on the goddess.* St. Paul, MN: Llewellyn Publications.

Mountainwater, S. (1991). *Ariadne's thread.* Freedom, CA: The Crossing Press.

NicMhacha, S. M. (2005). *Queen of the night: Rediscovering the Celtic moon goddess.* San Francisco, CA: Weiser Books.

Quarrie, D. (2010). *Dancing with the goddess.* CA: CreateSpace.

__(2010). *Annym billagh: healing with the tree ogham.* CA: CreateSpace.

__(2010). *From the Branch: The ogham for spiritual health.* CA: CreateSpace.

☽ ○ ☾

Stein, D. (1990). *Casting the circle: A woman's book of ritual.* Freedom, CA: Crossing Press.

__(2004). *Diane Stein's guide to goddess craft.* Freedom, CA: Crossing Press.

Walker, B. G. (1983). *The women's encyclopedia of myths and secrets.* New York: HarperCollins Publishers.

__(1988). *A woman's dictionary of symbols and sacred objects.* New York: HarperCollins Publishers.

__ (1988). *The crone: Woman of age, wisdom, and power.* New York: HarperCollins Publishers.

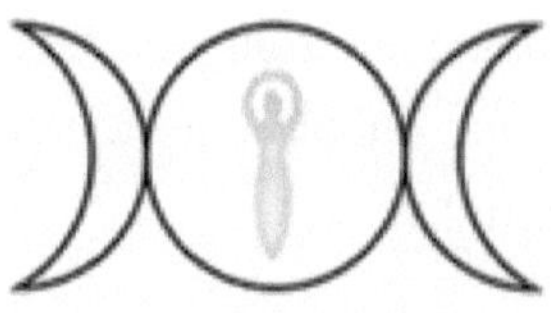

Appendix B

Liturgical Structure

Creating a ritual can be a fun and spontaneous process when you are working alone. When you are working in groups, it's generally a good idea to create a formal structure that can be easily applied through diverse occasions. It is like having an outline that everyone can follow, even if the details have changed. The structure of rituals vary among groups. The below structure and function are how I craft rituals and what was taught to me within liturgical classes that examined religious rituals across religious backgrounds. If you look at my suggested reading list, you'll find a host of texts on Goddess Rites to help inspire you whether you use the below structure or something different! At the conclusion of this, I've included a ritual I've utilized with students to explore these liturgical structures.

Invocation

This is the first part of your ritual where you welcome members to your communal rite and clearly define the purpose of the ritual. Purposing your rituals are important as it serves to ensure that not only is everyone participating understands what's going on, but that everyone's energy is directed toward the same goal. This also allows everyone to set aside their individual needs and personal issues through the day and to merge with the group to great a smooth working dynamic. By considering this as the welcoming portion of the rite, you also increase the positive and opening energy to create a safe, loving environment. An example of an invocation is: "Welcome friends to our Imbolc Rite; tonight we welcome the new born light within each of us."

Opening Meditation

Once everyone knows what the rite is about and feels settled in, it's time to help everyone focus their energy toward the rite's purpose. This also helps every transition out of the stress from their outside lives and begin to create a sacred mindset—this is where we all get to clear our hears. In most Neopagan circles, this is the moment in the ritual process where we ground and center ourselves. Consider a guided meditation that is infused with images of the ritual's underlying myths; a meditation that allows participants to visualize their own grounding in the Earth; ritual drumming, singing, or chanting are other modes for grounding and centering.

Opening & Consecration

Once everyone has a clear mind and heart, it's time to begin the sacred elements of the rite. This is where ritual symbols or the participants themselves are transformed from their mundane or everyday use/being into a sacred object/being. During the Consecration, the intention of the rite is restated—this is the part of the ritual where everything is spiritually *transformed* into the *holy.*

Casting the Circle, Calling the Quarters: The Transformation of Space

Ritual's purpose is to transform our consciousness and transport us to the liminal space. In Neopagan traditions this is done through circle-casting and quarter-calling. This creates a protected space designed to contain the energy of the participants and to create a spiritual-energetic pathway between them, the Divine, and other realms. Different traditions have different ways of engaging in this process.

☽ ○ ☾

Invocation of the Deity(ies)

Once the space and individuals participating have been sanctified, the chosen priestess invokes the Deity linked to the rite. This is often done through song or poetic expression or through ecstatic possession, whereby the Deity speaks through the priestess. I prefer spontaneity during this peak experience as this is generally the high-point of any rite. I also often encourage participants to feel the spirit and invoke as well as this raises energy and creates a more egalitarian group where all members participate to co-create the rite.

Offertory

After the deity has been invoked, the deity is said to be present within the circle. A sign of respect is to have an offering for the Deity in gratitude for the love they have shown and their help they will continue to give. Offerings are generally based on research into the mythic tradition of the Deity being invoked; I prefer to offer items from Nature that can be later left outside to continual give back to the world.

Concluding Prayer

After the offering a final prayer is given to the Divine invoked. This is a prayer that ideally reinforces the meaning of the rite that has been conducted. This allows participants to take time in reflection of the rite and to deepen their understanding of what has transpired. This is also the point in the ritual that action is taken on the part of the participants—in a working ritual, this would be where the magic would occur. Additionally, during this period of time wine, cakes, water, or bread are blessed and shared communally as a means of individuals becoming empowered with the energy of the Divine and to more deeply internalize the rite and to reinforce their inner divinity. This also helps strengthen the bonds of friendship and oneness through the sharing of food.

Benediction

This is the final invocation of the deity to reinforce the blessings sought.

☽ ○ ☾

Parting

Once the final blessing has been given and the final act of the rite completed the sacred space is ready to be disassembled. Participants give thanks to the Divine and part the energy. Then the quarters are thanked and undone, followed by the circle—until the sacred space has been returned to its earthy energy. At which time, participants once more acknowledge their fellowship and say a final blessing from themselves to each other. The priestess ideally gives a final thought that allows participants to return home feeling peace and compassion.

An Imbolc Ritual Example

Ritual Supplies

Quarter/Element symbols:

☽ Water dish for altar, set in the West
☽ Incense for altar, set in the East
☽ Sand dish for altar, set in the North
☽ 1 red candle for altar, set in the South

Center altar symbols

☽ 1 blue candle for altar (reflecting Spirit)
☽ 1 tan candle for altar (reflecting Earth)
☽ 1 white candle for altar (for the unified Deity, Male and Female)
☽ Athame and/or wand, I use a driftwood wand to symbolize the power of the elements which are joined by natural forces to create the wand.
☽ Chalice for water for altar to be passed to each participant during the reception of the blessing
☽ Pentacle for food for altar to be passed to each participant during the reception of the blessing
☽ Altar cloth

☽ ○ ☾

Imbolc altar symbols

- ☽ One central white candle to symbolize Brigid's light
- ☽ White candles for all participants
- ☽ Fresh white flowers and dried grasses to offer Brigid
- ☽ Basket for altar to hold flowers and symbolize the womb

Invocation

Welcome everyone to our Imbolc celebration.
Today we come together in celebration and honor of holy Queen and Mother Goddess Brigid,
as her presence returns to seed our world with new growth as Her Light returns.
She, the Exalted One, shall rise arise in our land as the brilliance of the shining sun.
She, the Exalted One, shall renew life through inspiration, regeneration, and healing.
We come together today to be nourished by her Holy Milk,
as it begins to break free from the Winter's icy chill to flow down into the valleys.

Opening Meditation

Let us take a moment to clear our minds and prepare our spirits.
Begin by taking several slow and deep breaths.
Allow the nourishing air to feed you, calm you, and still your minds.
Allow all thoughts of your everyday life to drift away with each exhalation.

Now imagine you are standing amidst a cool, snow covered valley.
The wind is crisp; the valley is silent and still.
It is a time of the deep winter, where the land is sleeping under a thick white blanket.

☽ ○ ☾

The evergreens rise tall, reaching the steel gray sky, a dark green against the snow-white background.
The maples, oaks, and willows stand thread-bare and exposed, with small seed pods barely perceptible dotting their limbs.
In the distance you hear the sound of water.
It is faint at first, but as the sun rises high overhead to warm your cheeks, the sound increases.
You follow the sound toward a brook; clear ice covers it, but you see that it is melting.
The shimmering glass of the ice is being transformed to living water as you watch.
And soon the sun's transformative heat unlocks the brook and water flows.
You bend low, no longer feeling the cold of the winter landscape,
and cup your hands into the cool water.
You splash your face and take a deep breath.
You feel refreshed.
You feel grounded.
You feel centered.
You feel purified by the sun-infused water.
Take a moment to allow yourself to soak up the cool water and feel the heat of the sun.

Opening & Consecration

In love and trust, we come together to perform the sacred rites of the Creative Force.
Our Mother and Father, our Lord and Lady, our Beginnings and our Endings,
the force that dwells in all of Nature and within each of us.

[holding up a Blue Candle]

In love and trust, we welcome the divine energy that is within each of us to our holy rites.

[lights the Blue Candle]

[holding up a Tan Candle]

In love and trust, we welcome the divine energy of Earth that envelopes us to our holy rites.

[lights the Tan Candle]

[holding up a White Candle]

In love and trust, we welcome the Creative Force, the union of the Divine Mother and Father, the spirit of birth, of death, and rebirth, to our holy rites.

[lights the White Candle]

Group Says: Blessed Be.

[holding up incense, using a driftwood wand makes the Air pentagram]

I consecrate you, Breath of Life, source of spirit and earthly life, the inspiration and expiration of the Divine Mother and Father.

Group Says: Blessed Be.

[holding up a red candle, using a driftwood wand makes the Fire pentagram]

I consecrate you, Energy of Life, transformative spark of spirit and earthly life, the passion and will of the Divine Mother and Father.

Group Says: Blessed Be.

[holding up a dish of water, using the driftwood wand makes the Water pentagram]

I consecrate you, Nourisher of Life, food of spirit and earthly life, the compassion and love of the Divine Mother and Father.

Group Says: Blessed Be.

[holding up a dish of sand, using the driftwood want makes the Mineral/ Earth pentagram]

I consecrate you, Rock of Life, foundation and form of spirit and earthly life, the strength and purpose of the Divine Mother and Father.

Group Says: Blessed Be.

Casting the Circle

We will now cast our circle to create our sacred space and secure our protection as we work together. Please repeat after me and visualize your own energy linking with each person.

[Raising driftwood wand and standing in the East to move clockwise around three times]

Group Says: With my Breath.

Group Says: With my Energy,

Group says: With my Compassion.,

☽ ○ ☾

Group Says: With my Strength of Purpose

Group Says: I craft this circle three times round

Group Says: To protect and unify My being with the Divine.

Group Says: May this sacred circle

Group Says: Be filled with love, trust, and peace.

Group Says: So do I will,

Group Says: So mote it be.

The circle is cast.

Calling of the Quarters

[Standing in the East, draws an invoking pentagram with driftwood wand and lights the incense, placing it in the eastern quarter]

Sylphs, nature spirits born of the Air,
Who reside in the sky and speak on the wind,
We call to you to share your wisdom and guard our work.
By the Breath of Life, come to us.

Group Says: Blessed Be.

[Standing in the South, draws an invoking pentagram with driftwood wand and lights the red candle, placing it in the southern quarter]

☽ ○ ☾

Salamanders, nature spirits born of Fire,
Who reside in the magma and speak in the volcanoes,
We call to you to share your passion and guard our work.
By the Energy of Life, come to us.

Group Says: Blessed Be.

[Standing in the West, draws an invoking pentagram with driftwood wand and holds the dish water up, placing it in the western quarter]

Undines, nature spirits born of Water,
Who reside in the oceans and speak in the tides,
We call to you to share your compassion and guard our work.
By the Nourisher of Life, come to us.

Group Says: Blessed Be.

[Standing in the North, draws an invoking pentagram with driftwood wand and holds up the dish of sand, placing it in the northern quarter]

Gnomes, nature spirits born of sand and stone,
Who reside in the deepest mountains and speak in streams of dust,
We call to you to share your steadfastness and guard our work
By the Rock of Life, come to us.

Group Says: Blessed Be.

We now stand between the worlds where all are joined and one.
We are linked to the Web of Life;
We have only one Spirit, Divine.
We have only one Body, Earth.
We have only one Feeling, Love.
We have only one Thought, Oneness.

☽ ○ ☾

Group Says: Blessed Be.

Message/Invocation of Brigid

[each participant should hold up their candle]

Mother–Queen Brigid, be with us and within us.

Group Says: Bless us and be blessed.

We carry within us your Divine Light,
which melts the snows of winter and begins to shine
offering a glimmer of Spring,
of renewed hope, healing, and inspiration.

Group Says: Bless us and be blessed.

[all light your candles]

We honor Brigid's Light, rising as the Sun.
The seeds buried deep beneath the cold ground quicken.
The Earth is awakening, Brigid arise
and be our Guide,
our Comforter,
and our Protector
as we worship you in our sacred space today,
and in our thoughts, actions, and relationships through your Season.

Group Says: Bless us and be blessed.

Offertory

[holding up a basket of fresh white flowers, seeds, and corn husks, to be

scattered outdoors after the ritual]

Holy Queen, Holy Mother Brigid,
Bringer of Healing, Rebirth, and Wisdom,
Goddess of the Quickening and Coming Spring,
We honor Your presence in our lives.
Accept our gift, knowing that it comes from our
Hearts, Minds, Bodies, and Spirit.

Group Says: Blessed Be

[holding up your own cup of water to drink from]

Bless our Water,
that we may be renewed.

[holding up edible seeds, fruits, bread or sweets to eat;
if you do not have this, you can definitely eat make a point to eat later to receive the blessing]

Bless our Food
that we may be fortified.

Group Says: So mote it be.

Concluding Prayer

Let us pray:

Brigid, young Bride of the Horned God,
of Faunus, and the Green Man,
You are the keeper of the eternal flame,
the Sun that never leaves us.

☽ ○ ☾

You have nourished the hearth of our world
through the Dreaming Time of Winter,
watching over us as we slept,
keeping us warm and secure.

You are Transformation,
The Fiery Forge that both splits and connects.
The seed breaks open in your flames,
and from its death, new life begins.

Group Says: Blessed Be

Benediction/Parting

[taking the drinking water that has been blessed]

We receive Your blessing in our lives.
May we be blessed with what nourishes us.

[drink]

[taking the food that has been blessed]

We receive Your blessing in our lives.
May we be blessed with what strengthens us.

[eat]

We thank you Brigid, Exalted One,
Goddess whom Inspiration has adored,
for being with us on this, Your holiest of days.

Group Says: In gratitude we say farewell.

☽ ○ ☾

[Standing in the North, drawing a banishing pentagram]

Gnomes, nature spirits born of sand and stone,
We thank you.

Group Says: By the Rock of Life, we say farewell.

[Standing in the West, drawing a banishing pentagram]

Undines, nature spirits born of Water,
We thank you.

Group Says: By the Nourisher of Life, we say farewell.

[Standing in the South, blows out the candle, drawing a banishing pentagram]

Salamanders, nature spirits born of Fire,
We thank you.

Group Says: By the Energy of Life, we say farewell.

[Standing in the East, puts out the incense, drawing a banishing pentagram]

Sylphs, nature spirits born of the Air,
We thank you.

Group Says: By the Breath of Life, we say farewell.

[holding Driftwood wand, I cut through the circle]

☽ ○ ☾

What has been crafted is now undone,
Spirits joined are now themselves once more.
Energies raised have returned to Mother Earth.
We are between the worlds no more.
Our circle is now open and our rites have ended.

Group Says: Merry Meet, Merry Part, and Merry Meet again.

☽ ○ ☾

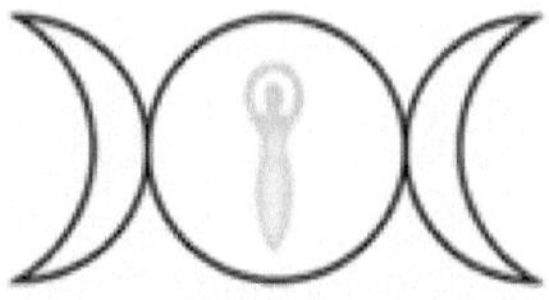

Notes

Chapter 1

1 Norse mythology, he is the snake that encircles the upper, middle, and lower world—the whole of universe—with his tail in his mouth, indicating the ending is the beginning.

2 Parthogenesis means the ability to procreate without a male partner. While there are no accounts of this ability occurring in human beings there is ample biological evidence from non-human species of this method of procreation.

3 I use the term "thealogy" versus "theology" as this reflects the study of the goddess or the divine feminine, rather than god. This also reflects a marked change in thinking, highlighting patriarchal influences within religion, whereby the study of the Divine was engendered as male and legitimized by academia, as well as religion as the only way of seeing, knowing, and experiencing the "Divine".

4 Natural cycles are often the primary sources for the establishment of religious holy days. Within Goddess traditions, these are particularly important as Nature is often conceptualized as the "body" of the Goddess, as well as natural cycles are seen as physical manifestations of how the Goddess develops.

5 A wonderful example of this is depicted in Shekhinah Mountainwater's *Ariadne's Thread*.

6 It is important to note that in religious history, the moon was just as likely to be associated with a male deity. The same is found with solar associations, which are now perceived as largely associated with male deities, but in fact were historically linked to divine females.

7 The Dark Moon is actually the New Moon—there is some confusion in Neopagan groups as to what this means. But the New Moon is astronomically known as the darkest period of time, right before the moon will reappear.

8 Wicca terms these as "esbats".

9 These dates are for Western Hemisphere only.

10 These were non-binding marriages that allowed young persons to determine whether or not they "fit" with the other individual before making a marital commitment.

11 Hecate interestingly was a handmaiden to Persephone, and thus a Maiden Goddess. However because her property as the Goddess of the Witches and the Crosroads; she is seen as the elder statesman.

12 see Dunlap, R. E. (1983). Ecologist versus exemptionalist: The Ehrlich –Simon debate. *Social Science Quarterly, 64,* 200–203.

13 Anthropocentrism and humancentrism mean the same thing: having a focus that revolves solely around human concerns. Within environmental philosophy, the goal is often to become an individual with an ecocentric perspective—that is having the capacity to recognize their relationship to and impact upon a wide ecological system that includes nonhumans. Ecofeminists, an environmental philosophy of critical importance for thealogians holds that the distancing and demonization of all creatures within Nature and the planet itself stems from androcentrism, that is frameworks in which the world revolves around men. However, within thealogy the maintenance of agrarian celebrations is particularly challenging as these run counter to an ecofeminist and ecocentric position. As at their core they highlight the management and manipulation of the Earth and nonhuman life to suit the needs of human beings, with the assumption that such actions are "natural" or "spiritual" rather than a recognition that they are largely human created. Two ex-

cellent sources to explore ecofeminism is Warren's *Ecofeminist Philosophy: A Western Perspective on What It Is and Why It Matters* and Diamond and Orenstein's *Reweaving the World: The Emergence of Ecofeminism.*

14 Western Hemisphere dates.

15 This is expanding somewhat, but remains a general lack in the field. One of the reasons is the general view that women, living in a patriarchal culture, need a faith that is solely their own to help them make meaning in a society that places them in second-class positions. Many Goddess adherents reject the notion men can fully understand the Goddess because of their valued position in society and they would potentially bring suppressive attitudes into the religious forum and thus women would be once more dislocated from a source of power. However, about three years ago I spoke with Z Budapest, the founding Mother of Dianic Witchcraft, regarding how she might adapt her own teachings to meet the needs of men who wish to know the Goddess, and she noted it was something she was considering more and more in her Crone years. Nevertheless, it still remains a missing element with the "male" role seen as a secondary creation of the Goddess. It is something that emerging thealogians may wish to tackle.

6 Men actually do go through menopause similar to women, that includes emotional and physical changes brought about by a drop in testosterone and reproduction capacity.

Chapter 2

1 Wilshire, D. (1994). *Virgin Mother Crone: Myths & mysteries of the triple goddess.* Rochester, VT: Inner Traditions International, Ltd. p. 49

2 Shamans, L. (2009). Aphrodite and ecology: The goddess of love as nature archetype. *Ecopsychology,* 1, 93–97. p. 94

3 Have each member do their own finger with their own rose.

☽ ○ ☾

Chapter 3

1 Cunningham, N. B. (1995). *I am woman by rite: A book of women's rituals.* York Beach, Maine: Samuel Weiser, Inc. p. 47

2 Shekhinah Mountainwater suggests to truly understand the Maiden goddess, we must look at her as having a double aspect: the Bright Maiden and the Dark Maiden. This makes enormous lunar sense given the double-aspect Goddess is symbolized by the waxing (building) crescent moon and the waning (leaving) crescent moon. While the Mother is manifested in the Full Moon and the Crone is manifested in the New Moon (dark of the moon).

3 Budapest, Z. E. (1991). *Grandmother Moon: Lunar magic in our lives.* San Francisco: HarperCollins Publishers. p. 11

4 *abers* refers to the mouth of a river.

5 *coracles* an arcane word for coral and coral-like species.

6 an unknown British-Isle warlord.

7 wondering in this context refers to an older meaning of literal wonderment or awe, rather than confusion or questioning as it means in contemporary terms.

8 Gwydyon, a bardic magician in Celtic lore.

9 A majority of Celtic literature that survives detailing pre-Christian beliefs comes to us from preservation by Christian Monks. In these early works we often see the merging of or the side-by-side tolerance of pagan practices with Christian ones, prior to more widespread assimilation of Christian beliefs. This poem is no different, merging the magical practices and animistic beliefs of the prior Celtic-based belief system with Christian imagery. Robert Graves interpretation of this poem was to reduce it to about 48 lines, excluding most of the text's narrative to only examine the rising of the trees, which he felt reflected more of the non-Christian core truths of the poem. The challenge of this editorial stripping is that the context of the rising up of the trees becomes obscured. I've chosen to provide you with the entire text. While this makes for a

reading that is jarring—this reflects the likely experiences of the composer of the poem in a time when a cohesive religion was not visible. It is also important to note that the narrator of the poem, the Taliessin is not Christian—he is referring to Christian people, "the Lord answered them" and the Lord would "deliver those whom he made"—all of which implies the author of the poem adhered to an older tradition (as also reinforced by the author's own shape-shifting presence). We also find the Christian people are asked to go into battle and be like trees—our author will actually bring to life trees, suggesting a definitive statement of the author's spiritual power versus the imitational power of these people. They can only be *like* the way they were; further the imitational element disturbs the trees themselves who rise up and reassert balance and truth. However, it is also important to note that within early Christian British Isle literature the tree was considered a profoundly important spiritual figure linked to the Cross of Crucifixion, whereby the tree is sentient and alive, aware of its role as the bridge between life and death—which may reflect the acquisition of Druidic or early pagan beliefs and their own associations of trees as spiritually potent bridges between the living world and the dead; something re-examined when the Alder tree is mentioned. This is further consistent with widespread shamanistic beliefs in the World Tree through which individuals utilize to journey to upper and lower spiritual landscapes.

10 The "sleepless cow" is likely a secondary reference to the female who appears to quell the din. This likely refers to a goddess figure. Cows were widely utilized in antiquity as symbolic of Goddesses—who are capable of nurturing the world and bringing into life new modes of existence. What we find is this nurturing, peaceful, mother of all creatrix does not sway the war-mongering energy of the battle-ready men.

11 see the "Book of Aneurin".

12 Here we again return to the notion that our writer pre-dates Christian tradition and the ninth wave is an interesting allusion that is shared with Heimdall of Norse mythology. A primordial son who is the "bridge" between worlds, similar to Bran the Blessed within Celtic lore, and the

father of the human race and he son of nine waves.
13 Math was a magician-god who created Blodeuwedd, the Goddess of Spring, with Gwydyon, another magician who rescues, Lleu, the cursed son of Arianrhod.
14 These are genealogical descriptions and likely referring back to Math and Gwydyon—the first reference is obscure and unknown. Modron is typically a mother goddess figure often associated with Rhiannon.
15 Arthur, likely a reference to King Arthur.
16 Dylan is the son of the wave, notably the second wave of Arianrhod—another of her children.
17 *canhwr* refers to an arcane military Roman term meaning 100 men in a military unit. In this phrase it would indicate nine military units. As such, the writer is merging the mythic with the actual, describing in vivid detail in the preceding 10 lines an encounter with a relatively large standing army.
18 Liturgical vestments typically worn during Christian communion.
19 Blodeuwedd's lover who ultimately kills Lleu.
20 We have three Biblical demarcations noted here: the flood, the crucifixion, and the final judgment.
21 This is an obscure conclusion to the poem, but it likely suggests being freed from a mortal life. In Celtic lore, Govannon was said to be the deity of smith-work and through him, individuals could obtain a goblet that granted immortality. Other interpretations suggest the last word was the Welsh word for Virgil and this associated with the transformative goddess Cerridwen. We also find in the last few lines a very resplendent sense of self as the poet declares their own value and utilizes the word "wanton" suggesting a flaunting against Christian ideals. This conclusion is somewhat abrupt as it is the only time that the author speaks directly to an audience—in this case a non-Christian one, making the Christianized elements of the text feel that much more awkward.
22 There are numerous Christian overtones to Dylan's story, whereby he is baptized in water and transformed into a fish until he is sacrificed within a later mythic cycle. This indicates a privileging of this figure as

redemptive and similar to Christ in the Celtic tradition during its merging with Christianity. It also indicates a more wider tradition in human mythology of resurrecting sons of great Goddesses who give birth without the need for men.

Chapter 4

1 From Ben Johnson's "Hymn to Diana." The entire text reads as follows:
Queen and huntress, chaste and fair,
Now the sun is laid to sleep,
Seated in thy silver chair
State in wonted manner keep:
Hesperus entreats thy light,
Goddess excellently bright.
Earth, let not thy envious shade
Dare itself to interpose;
Cynthia's shining orb was made
Heaven to clear when day did close:
Bless us then with wished sight,
Goddess excellently bright.
Lay thy bow of pearl apart
And thy crystal-shining quiver;
Give unto the flying hart
Space to breath, how short soever:
Thou that makest a day of night,
Goddess excellently bright.

2 The Athenians utilized the Attic calendar, which was a Lunar calendar that begins on the first New Moon after the Summer Solstice, known as the month of Hekatombaion. The celebration in honor of Artemis each month would follow as the 6th day after each New Moon.

3 I prefer the term Grotto, which not only evokes the idea of sacred places embedded within nature, but also simultaneously means

"concealed" or "hidden" place, thus reflecting the mystery of Goddess worship—its mystical elements.

Chapter 5

1 Quarrie, D. (2008). *From the branch: A primer in Dianic Witchcraft.* USA: Lulu Press. p. 6

2 Creation is embodied by either or both creativity and procreativity. To connect with and be embodied by Creatrix means to manifest all of one's potential, whether one becomes a literal mother/father or not. In other words the Creatrix does not limit our potential based on biological fertility.

3 One way to re-envision this myth is to consider Persephone as the Maiden aspect of Demeter—that they are in fact one.

4 In Goddess-based traditions all individuals who come to know the Goddess are seen as priest and priestess.

Chapter 6

1 Cunningham, N. B. (1995). *I am woman by rite: The book of women's rituals.* York Beach, ME: Samuel Weiser, Inc. p.52

2 Budapest, Z. (1991). *Grandmother moon: Lunar magic in our lives.* San Francisco: HarperCollins Publishers. p. 10.

3 Her text, *Grandmother Moon,* is highly recommended for her insights and interpretations of each moon, along with a compendium of Moon-related Goddess festivals that might be integrated into a mythic calendar.

4 It is not uncommon for groups who work together for long periods of time also experience the Moon phases similarly in terms of Moontales and tides. This is in keeping with our natural tendency to mirror each other in small bands, as we did in our ancient primeval lives. It is also reflects the shared connection we have with each other and is similar to why women who live together often begin to attune their menstrual cy-

cles together (another symbol of the Moon).

5 For further Goddess moon references, consider picking up a copy of *Moonscapes: A celebration of lunar astronomy, magic, legend, and lore* by Rosemary Ellen Guiley.

6 see Matthews, C. (1989). *The elements of the Celtic tradition.* Rockport, MA: Element Books Limited.

Chapter 7

1 Ochshorn, J. (1997). Goddesses and the lives of women. In K. L. King (Ed), *Woman and Goddess Traditions: In Antiquity and Today* (pp. 377–399). Minneapolis, MN: Fortress Press. p 387

2 *Shakti* is term for the supreme Goddess; shaktism is a cultic worship of the Goddess and a subgroup of Hinduism.

3 Erndl, K. M. (1997). The goddess and women's power: A Hindu case study. In K. L. King (Ed), *Woman and Goddess Traditions: In Antiquity and Today* (pp. 17–38). Minneapolis, MN: Fortress Press. p. 20

Chapter 8

1 Crone Goddesses were traditionally symbolized by large polished stones, which were covered in embroidered cloths to prevent adherents from directly touching or viewing them.

2 Menstrual blood was seen as a magical source of power and, remains a powerful source of power in contemporary Goddess paths; Crones no longer menstruating were believed to contain their menstrual blood within them and this gave them supernatural and magical powers.

3 Walker, B.G. (1985). *The Crone: Woman of age, wisdom, and power.* New York: Harper & Row. p. 29.

Chapter 9

1 Mountainwater, S. (1991). *Ariadne's thread.* Freedom, CA: The Crossing Press.

2 Some goddess workers hold the New Moon is the "dark goddess" when they interpret this to mean the Crone. For the purposes of our discussion and thealogical consistency, the Dark Goddess refers to the waning crescent, thus counterbalancing the Maiden.

3 p. 65, *Ariadne's Thread*

4 This refers to not only seeing what is physical, but also the intuitive capacity to see what lies beneath and beyond.

5 see George, D. (1992). *Mysteries of the dark moon: The healing power of the Dark Goddess.* New York: HaperCollins Publishers.

6 ibid p. 28

7 Budapest, Z. (2003). *The holy book of women's mysteries.* San Francisco, CA: Weiser Books. (Original publication 1980). p.8

☽ ○ ☾

About the Author

Dr. Katherine MacDowell has had a rich and varied professional and educational background. She holds multiple graduate degrees in psychology and in theology. She has extensively studied Feminist Thealogy and spent two years immersed at the Women's Spirituality Forum under the direction of Z. Budapest. Her primary research focus is in the atheistic philosophical system of Religious Naturalism and the relationship between religion and the environmental crisis. She is an ordained interfaith minister and shamanic teacher. She is also widely published in academic journals within the field of ecopsychology and environmentalism. She is the host of the online radio program Eco-Chat, focused on ecospirituality, ecopsychology, and environmental action.

Outside of her academic life, she has spent more than 8 years as a professional psychotherapist and addictions counselor and has lectured widely as a professional development provider for the New Jersey Department of Education. She is an award-winning produced playwright and a produced singer-songwriter and orchestral composer. She is the author of two poetry collections *Witness* and *Vestiges and Bones*.

After being diagnosed with a progressive disease that forced her into early retirement, she founded Ocean Seminary College to encourage global, multifaith seminary education that is barrier free (tuition-free, online with a mixture of self-study and group courses) coupled with the Grotto of Sacred Naturalism, a multifaith religious organization. To learn more, please visit:

www.KateEMacDowell.com
www.OceanSeminaryCollege.org

www.ingramcontent.com/pod-product-compliance
Ingram Content Group UK Ltd.
Pitfield, Milton Keynes, MK11 3LW, UK
UKHW041945190726
13854UKWH00004B/1805

9 780557 363506